ML
641.824 V887
Vollstedt, Maryana
Meatloaf : recipes for everyone's

P9-CDM-068

meat**LOAF**

WITHDRAWN

meatLOAF

RECIPES FOR EVERYONE'S FAVORITE

Maryana Vollstedt

PHOTOGRAPHS BY

JENNIFER LEVY

CHRONICLE BOOKS

SAN FRANCISCO

Text copyright © 2007 by
Maryana Vollstedt.
Photographs copyright © 2007
by Jennifer Levy.

All rights reserved. No part of this book
may be reproduced in any form without
written permission from the publisher.

LIBRARY OF CONGRESS
CATALOGING-IN-PUBLICATION
DATA AVAILABLE.

ISBN-10: 0-8118-4717-9
ISBN-13: 978-0-8118-4717-9

Manufactured in China

Designed and typeset by
Lucinda Hitchcock
This book was typeset in Egyptienne,
Gotham, Rosewood, and Snell.

Distributed in Canada by
Raincoast Books
9050 Shaughnessy Street
Vancouver, British Columbia V6P 6E5

10 9 8 7 6 5 4 3 2 1

Chronicle Books LLC
680 Second Street
San Francisco, California 94107
www.chroniclebooks.com

FOND DU LAC PUBLIC LIBRAR

641.824
V887

dedication

As always, I dedicate this book to my husband, Reed, who is my advisor, agent, shopper, tester, computer person, confidant, and best friend. He has encouraged and supported me throughout my many years of writing cookbooks. It has really been a team effort, and I couldn't have written them without him. Thank you, Reed. Also to my daughter, Julie Glogau, who tested some of the recipes and her husband, Tom, who was a happy taster.

acknowledgments

Thanks again to Bill LeBlond, editorial director of cookbooks at Chronicle Books, for his support and encouragement for me to continue to write cookbooks. *Meatloaf* is my eighth cookbook for Chronicle Books, following my titles in the best-selling Big Book series (*The Big Book of Easy Suppers, The Big Book of Potluck, The Big Book of Breakfast, The Big Book of Soups & Stews,* and *The Big Book of Casseroles*), plus two others, *Pacific Fresh* and *What's for Dinner?* To Amy Treadwell, associate editor at Chronicle Books, for always being available for help and advice during the writing of the book; to Carrie Bradley for her expert copyediting, additions, and suggestions; and all the staff at Chronicle Books. Also thanks to Mike Wooley, owner of Longs Meat Market in Eugene, Oregon, for his advice and quality meats. Special thanks to Brian Crow for his professional computer consulting and for developing my Web site, **www.maryana vollstedt.com**, and also for tasting recipes while on the job.

table of CONTENTS

JUST ABOUT **EVERYONE** *loves a meatloaf*

It is hearty, satisfying, nutritious, and homey, often bringing back happy memories when the fragrant, browned, and juicy loaf is presented at the table. Meatloaf has been a favorite in many countries for years, reportedly first appearing in this country toward the end of the nineteenth century. It has since become a family dining staple and an American classic, appealing to all ages. And with the renewed interest in comfort food, great homemade meatloaf is more popular than ever, and is often featured on the menu of upscale restaurants.

Though pleasing to the palate and offering complex layers of flavor, meatloaf is simplicity itself: a mixture of ground meat, starch, binder, liquid, vegetables, and seasonings made into a loaf and baked in the oven. Derived from traditional English meat-and-bread pudding and the renowned pâtés of France, the preparation is extremely versatile, lending itself well to a wide range of meats (as well as poultry and fish), vegetables, cheeses, herbs, spices, and other ingredients. A perfect meatloaf is a balance of ingredients that yields a tender yet firm loaf, with a blend of matching flavors.

In this book you will find an exciting selection of meatloaves for serving family and friends, with easy-to-find ingredients and straightforward directions. Featured here are recipes for all types of loaves, from rustic to sophisticated, classic to ethnic-inspired and other new creative combinations, along with sauces and toppings. In addition, there is a chapter featuring delicious variations — poultry, seafood, and vegetarian loaves — and another on complementary side dishes. Also included are helpful tips for preparing, baking, and serving meatloaf, and suggestions throughout for accompaniments.

Far from being limited to a single definitive recipe, meatloaf offers many possibilities for flavorful combinations and tempting sauces. I hope you enjoy the exciting array of choices in *Meatloaf,* and reach for this book whenever you need delicious and easy-to-prepare recipes that will please family or a crowd and add variety to your meal planning.

THE MAIN INGREDIENTS OF MEATLOAF

Meatloaves are a simple combination of meat, filler (starch), binder (egg), moistener (liquid), and flavorings (herbs, spices, ketchup, etc.). Toppings and sauces are often added for extra flavor and eye appeal.

MEATS Ground meats — *beef, veal, pork, sausage, ham,* and *lamb* — are the mainstay and body of the traditional meatloaf. Meatloaf can be made with one meat, or with a combination of meats for a more complex flavor. For best results, quality meats should be used. The standard proportion is 1 pound of ground beef and ½ pound of another meat, typically ground pork, but the meats and proportions are interchangeable. This amount will fit into an average size 9-by-5-inch loaf pan and will serve 4 to 6 people. Some meat markets offer a meatloaf mix of equal portions of beef for flavor and texture, pork for succulence, and veal for smoothness. You can make your own mix using a food processor to grind the meat, but do not overprocess or the meatloaf will be too dense.

Beef Ground beef chuck. For best results, use lean meat with about 15 percent fat. Do not use extra-lean, as some fat is needed to enhance the flavor and prevent the meatloaf from drying out.

Pork Ground pork, ground pork sausage, and *link sausage.* Ground pork is all pork without seasonings. Pork sausage has seasonings and some fat added. Italian sausage has Italian seasonings added and is available mild or hot. Various types of link sausages (such as kielbasa, chorizo, andouille, and others) can be added for extra-spicy flavor.

Ground lamb and *Veal* These may be available fresh at your supermarket or butcher shop, or can be purchased frozen. If any frozen meat is used, thaw thoroughly in the refrigerator and pat dry with a paper towel.

Game Ground venison and buffalo are now appearing in some markets and can be substituted for other meats.

POULTRY AND SEAFOOD Ground turkey and ground chicken have recently become popular, offering leaner versions of the traditional meatloaf mixes. Cooked or canned salmon or other firm cooked fish, such as halibut or snapper, can also be used in a loaf.

VEGETARIAN BASES A mixture of vegetables, beans or other legumes, and/or cereal and nuts as the base for loaves will appeal to the vegetarian or to those on special diets.

FILLERS The main purpose of "fillers," or the starch ingredients in a meatloaf mixture, is not to stretch the meat or the food-buying dollar, but to give the loaf body and texture and to absorb the flavorful juices. The most common filler is bread crumbs, either fresh or dried. Dried bread crumbs, in both fine and coarse grinds, are readily available in packages, in a range of styles and flavors — Progresso is an excellent brand, or the light and fluffy *panko* (Japanese bread crumbs, found in Asian markets and well-stocked supermarkets) are a reliable choice. Different breads (also found in some packaged crumbs), such as whole wheat, rye, pumpernickel, sourdough, cornbread, pita, challa, and focaccia, contribute their unique flavor and texture to the meatloaf. Other common fillers are crushed crackers; quick-cooking oats or other dry cereal; crushed tortilla chips; cooked rice, lentils or beans, pasta or potatoes; or instant grits or bulgur.

It's also easy to make your own bread crumbs, which can be very handy when you're caught without any in the pantry, and also enables you to experiment with any bread you like. One bread slice will make about 1 cup of crumbs.

To make fresh bread crumbs, trim crusts from bread slices, if desired, tear into large pieces, and process in a food processor or blender into coarse or fine crumbs.

To make dried bread crumbs, spread the fresh bread crumbs on a baking sheet and let dry in a 200°F oven for about 20 minutes or on the counter overnight.

If not using immediately, store all bread crumbs in a tightly covered container in the refrigerator for up to 1 week or in the freezer for up to 6 months.

To crush saltines or other crackers, place crackers in a zippered plastic bag and crush with a rolling pin or jar.

MOISTENER Milk, soup, juice, broth, cottage cheese, sour cream, yogurt, wine, gravy, barbecue sauce, and other sauces are used to keep the loaf tender and moist.

BINDER Eggs are generally used as a binder to hold the meatloaf together. One egg is usually sufficient for 1 to 1½ pounds of meat, 2 eggs for 2 pounds of meat. If you prefer, you can substitute 2 egg whites or ¼ cup egg substitute for 1 egg. The unbeaten eggs can be mixed with all of the ingredients at once or lightly beaten before adding to the mixture. Beating the eggs incorporates air and may make a lighter meatloaf.

FLAVORING Onions are the most commonly used ingredient to add flavor. Other flavorings include garlic, celery, mushrooms, carrots, and tomatoes. Some cooks prefer to sauté the vegetables first, but most vegetables, if finely chopped, will cook in the 1 hour baking time for the assembled loaf. Leftover cooked vegetables in your refrigerator are a handy option, too. For extra flavor and zest, ingredients such as ketchup, chili sauce, Worcestershire sauce, Tabasco sauce, mustard, horseradish, bacon bits, capers, herbs, spices, salt, and pepper can be added to the mix.

TOPPINGS, GLAZES, AND SAUCES Toppings and glazes are used to add flavor and color and help keep the meatloaf moist while baking. Sauces may be added at presentation or passed at the table. Follow the recipe directions for these enhancements, or create your own.

GARNISHES Garnishes, though optional, give the meatloaf a finishing touch, adding color and interest. Some choices are parsley, cilantro, watercress, cherry tomatoes, bell pepper strips, baby vegetables, fruit slices or wedges, mushrooms, pickles, olives, nuts, hard-cooked eggs, and even edible flowers.

WHY YOU'LL LOVE **MEATLOAF**

1. It's economical — one loaf serves 4 to 6 diners.
2. It's versatile, suitable for both family meals and casual entertaining.
3. It's easy to make and easy to serve.
4. It can be assembled ahead of time and refrigerated before baking; it also freezes well for longer storage.
5. It cooks in about an hour without further attention.
6. It's nutritional — it supplies a complete protein and is rich in calcium, iron, and other minerals.
7. It's equally good hot or cold (leftover meatloaf makes delicious sandwiches).
8. It's convenient — make an oven meal by baking potatoes or a casserole alongside.
9. It adds variety to meal planning.
10. It's reliable, with almost guaranteed good results from kitchen to table.

SPECIAL DIET TIPS

Adjustments can be made in the ingredients for the recipes in this book to fit diet requirements:

Substitute *ground turkey or chicken for beef to reduce the fat.*

Use *tomato paste instead of ketchup to reduce the salt.*

Use *low-fat cheese, tofu, or cottage cheese when cheese is called for.*

Use *high-fiber, low-fat bread crumbs.*

Substitute *skim milk for whole milk.*

Use *low-fat or fat-free, low-sodium broth.*

Use *reduced-sodium soy sauce.*

Reduce *the salt called·for in the recipe or use light salt.*

EQUIPMENT FOR MAKING MEATLOAF

The equipment for making meatloaf is simple and probably on hand in your kitchen, but read on for pan options for a variety of presentations.

MIXING

You'll need a large bowl, about a 3-quart capacity.

Clean hands are simply the best tool for mixing, or you can use two forks or a large spoon. A food processor can also be used to combine all the ingredients, but care must be taken not to overprocess, or the meatloaf will have a dense texture, as in a pâté.

BAKING CONTAINERS

A nonstick metal, enameled-lined, or glass 9-by-5-inch loaf pan is generally used for 1½ pounds of meat, or a 10-by-5-inch loaf pan for 2-pound loaves. Foil pans can also be used for easy serving and cleanup.

Use small foil tins for individual loaves, or cupcake tins for mini loaves.

Baking dishes, cake pans, casseroles, or cast-iron skillets can be used for free-form molded loaves. Some cooks prefer hand-molded meatloaves because they are firmer, the fat drains off in the extra space, and they have a crustier exterior. Molded loaves are typically round or oval, with the top either mounded or smoothed flat. Square or rectangular baking dishes can also be used to make square loaves; cut into squares to serve.

Ring molds make an attractive presentation, with vegetables or mashed potatoes mounded in the center hole at serving after the mold is removed.

Special meatloaf pans are available, fitted with a perforated insert that allows the grease to drip off (although with today's leaner meats, this is usually not necessary).

It is fun to vary the shape of meatloaf for serving by using different pans.

Use cooking spray or oil to lightly coat all containers before use.

THE **BASIC STEPS** IN MAKING A MEATLOAF

1. READ THE RECIPE and be sure you have all of the ingredients on hand and assembled for use. Place all the ingredients in a large bowl and mix as directed, or, if you prefer, whisk the egg first, then add the remaining ingredients.

2. GENTLY MIX ALL THE INGREDIENTS together with clean hands, two forks, or a large spoon, scooping up from the bottom of the bowl and lightly tossing and turning until well blended; do not overmix. To keep the meat from sticking to your hands, rinse them in cold water before mixing.

3. TURN THE MIXTURE into a lightly sprayed or oiled pan and gently pat down, but do not pack. Some cooks prefer to mound the top in the traditional meatloaf style. Leave ½ inch at the top of the pan to allow for glazes and toppings, if called for. See page 16 for baking pan suggestions.

4. IF MAKING AHEAD, cover the meatloaf in the pan tightly with aluminum foil or plastic wrap and refrigerate for up to 1 day or freeze for up to 1 month. If frozen, let thaw in the refrigerator before baking (about 24 hours) or allow 20 to 30 minutes extra baking time. (Most of the recipes in this book can be doubled to make an extra loaf.) Add any glazes or toppings at baking time or when called for.

5. PREHEAT THE OVEN to 350°F. Bake for about 1 hour for an average 9-by-5-inch meatloaf, or until an instant-read thermometer inserted in the center of the meatloaf registers 160°F. Larger meat-loaves will take about 10 minutes longer.

6. **WHEN THE MEATLOAF IS DONE,** remove from the oven and drain off any liquid in the pan that may have accumulated. With today's leaner meats, this may not be necessary, but you may find some rendered fat when pork sausage is included in the loaf. Let the meatloaf stand for 5 to 10 minutes in the pan to allow the juices to redistribute and the flavors to develop; it will also be firmer for easier slicing.

7. **TO REMOVE THE MEATLOAF** from a metal or glass pan, run a knife around the edges and gently lift to release the loaf from the pan. To remove from a foil pan, snip the sides of the pan with kitchen scissors and slide the meatloaf onto a serving plate; discard the pan. To serve, transfer the meatloaf to a cutting board and slice, then arrange on a platter or individual plates. Fancy meatloaves with a special topping are usually served whole on a decorative platter and garnished for an attractive presentation.

8. **ADD GARNISH,** if desired; see suggestions (page 14).

9. **SERVE WITH SAUCES,** if called for.

10. **PROMPTLY COVER** and refrigerate any leftover meatloaf and use within a few days. Meatloaves make wonderful sandwiches the next day.

MEATLOAVES

Tired of serving the same old boring, brown meatloaf over and over again? Try some of the exciting new meatloaves featured in this chapter and you will impress your family and friends.

Choose from diverse renditions such as:

- *Truck-Stop Meatloaf with Sausage Gravy and Baking Powder Biscuits*
- *Bloody Mary Meatloaf*
- *Pizza Meatloaf*
- *Breakfast Meatloaf Benedict*
- *Bill's Thai Meatloaf with Chili Sauce*
- *Mexican Meatloaf with Corn and Chipotle Mayonnaise*
- *Bistro Meatloaf*

plus many exciting sauces and toppings.

CLASSIC MEATLOAF

Serves 4 to 6   *This basic recipe is my version of the essential meatloaf. You can vary the recipe as you like — for example, by using extra garlic or hot-pepper sauce, replacing the bell pepper with additional onion, or using a mixture of fresh herbs — but this is a "blueprint" for the well-loved classic. Fluffy Mashed Potatoes (page 91) with butter floating on top are the natural side dish, for a perfect comfort-food plate.*

1   pound ground beef
½   pound ground pork sausage
½   cup finely chopped yellow onion
½   cup finely chopped red or green
      bell pepper
2   tablespoons chopped
      fresh parsley
2   garlic cloves, minced
¾   cup dried bread crumbs
1   large egg, lightly beaten
¼   cup whole milk
3   tablespoons ketchup
1   teaspoon prepared yellow
      mustard
1   teaspoon Worcestershire sauce
2   or 3 drops Tabasco
      or other hot-pepper sauce
½   teaspoon salt
¼   teaspoon freshly ground
      pepper
      Parsley sprigs for garnish

Preheat the oven to 350°F. In a large bowl, combine all the ingredients except the parsley sprigs, and mix well. Turn the mixture into a lightly sprayed or oiled 9-by-5-inch loaf pan and gently pat down. Bake until the loaf is firm and the top is lightly browned, about 1 hour. Let stand in the pan for 5 to 10 minutes before serving. Remove the loaf from the pan and slice to serve. Garnish with the parsley sprigs.

MOM'S MEATLOAF *with tomato sauce*

You can't beat mom's best meatloaf, full of home-cooked flavor and served with a sweet, tangy tomato sauce. Add baked potatoes to the menu for a cozy, family meal.

1   pound ground beef

½   pound ground pork sausage

½   cup finely chopped green
     bell pepper

½   cup finely chopped
     yellow onion

1   cup finely crushed saltines
     (about 20)

¼   cup ketchup

1   large egg, lightly beaten

½   teaspoon salt

¼   teaspoon freshly ground
     pepper

     Mom's Tomato Sauce (recipe
     follows) for serving

     Parsley sprigs for garnish

makes
about 1 cup

Preheat the oven to 350°F. In a large bowl, combine all the ingredients except the tomato sauce and parsley and mix well. Turn the mixture into a lightly sprayed or oiled 9-by-5-inch loaf pan and gently pat down. Bake until the loaf is firm and the top is lightly browned, about 1 hour. Let stand in the pan for 5 to 10 minutes before serving. Remove the loaf from the pan and transfer to a platter. Pour the hot tomato sauce over and garnish with the parsley sprigs.

Serves 6

MOM'S TOMATO SAUCE

This supremely easy tomato sauce is also suitable for pasta, in casseroles, or with other meats.

1   can (8 ounces) tomato sauce

1   tablespoon honey

1   teaspoon Worcestershire sauce

1   teaspoon red wine vinegar

½   teaspoon freshly ground pepper

In a small saucepan over medium heat, combine all the ingredients. Cook until the flavors are blended, about 5 minutes.

TRUCK-STOP MEATLOAF

WITH SAUSAGE GRAVY AND

baking powder biscuits

Serves 6 *After I asked my daughter to test two vegetarian loaves, her husband said, "Tell your mom to give us a man's loaf to test." Here it is. This hearty meatloaf served with Hash Browns (page 98) and Baking Powder Biscuits and Sausage Gravy will please any man — and women and children too!*

1½ pounds ground pork sausage

½   cup chopped yellow onion

¾   cup quick-cooking oats

½   cup tomato juice

1   large egg, lightly beaten

¼   teaspoon salt

¼   teaspoon freshly ground
     pepper

     Sausage Gravy (page 26)
     for serving

     Baking Powder Biscuits
     (page 27) for serving

Preheat the oven to 350°F. In a large bowl, combine all the ingredients except the gravy and biscuits and mix well. Turn the mixture into a lightly sprayed or oiled 9-by-5-inch loaf pan and gently pat down. Bake until the loaf is firm and the top is lightly browned, about 1 hour. Pour off any accumulated juices into a heatproof cup and reserve for the gravy. Let the loaf stand in the pan while you make the gravy, then remove from the pan and slice to serve. Serve with the gravy over the biscuits.

continued

SAUSAGE GRAVY

¼ pound ground pork sausage

1 thick bacon strip, diced

  Butter, if needed

3 tablespoons all-purpose flour

1 ½ cups whole milk

  Salt and freshly ground pepper

In a medium skillet over medium-high heat, sauté the sausage and bacon, breaking up the sausage with a spoon, until pink is no longer showing in the sausage and the bacon is crisp, 6 to 7 minutes. Transfer to a plate, leaving the drippings in the pan. Add butter, if needed, to make 3 tablespoons fat. Add the flour and whisk to blend. Add the milk, any reserved juices from the meatloaf, and whisk until the gravy is thickened, about 2 minutes. Return the sausage and bacon to the pan. Season with salt and pepper to taste.

makes about 2 cups

BAKING POWDER BISCUITS

These tender biscuits are easy enough to add to any menu— breakfast, lunch, or topped with berries and whipped cream for dessert.

2   cups all-purpose flour

1   tablespoon baking powder

1   teaspoon sugar

½   teaspoon salt

5   tablespoons cold unsalted
      butter or shortening,
      cut into pieces

¾ cup milk

Preheat the oven to 450°F. In a medium bowl, stir together the flour, baking powder, sugar, and salt. Using a pastry blender or 2 knives, cut in the butter until the mixture resembles coarse crumbs. Add the milk all at once and stir with a fork or wooden spoon until the mixture holds together. Gather the dough into a ball. Turn the dough out onto a lightly floured work surface and knead for about 30 seconds; do not overmix or the biscuits will be tough. Pat or roll the dough with a floured rolling pin into a circle ½ inch thick. Cut out biscuits with a floured 2½-inch biscuit cutter or a drinking glass.

Place on an ungreased baking sheet 1 inch apart for crusty biscuits, closer together for biscuits with soft sides. Gather up the scraps, roll out, and cut into additional biscuits. Bake until golden brown, about 12 minutes. Serve immediately.

makes 10 to 12 biscuits

EVERYDAY **MEATLOAF**

Serves 4 to 6 — *One friend of mine says this is her all-time favorite meatloaf for an easy supper, because although it's simple as any main dish can be, it will feed her large family and still leave leftovers for sandwiches.*

2 pounds ground beef

1 cup chopped yellow onion

1 cup fine dried bread crumbs

2 large eggs, lightly beaten

½ cup beef broth

3 tablespoons dry red wine

2 teaspoons Worcestershire sauce

½ teaspoon salt

¼ teaspoon freshly ground pepper

1 can (8 ounces) tomato sauce, divided

Preheat the oven to 350°F. In a large bowl, combine all the ingredients except the tomato sauce. Add 2 tablespoons of the tomato sauce and mix well. Turn the mixture into a lightly sprayed or oiled 10-by-5-inch loaf pan and gently pat down. Pour the remaining tomato sauce over. Bake until the loaf is firm and the sauce is bubbly, about 1 hour. Let stand in the pan for 5 to 10 minutes before serving. Remove the loaf from the pan and slice to serve.

SUPER **CHEESEBURGER** LOAF

Serves 6 *Your family will love this fine-textured meatloaf adapted from a favorite burger, and there's no mess from frying or grilling. Serve with Oven French Fries (page 96) to complete this rendition of the old-time drive-in combination.*

1¼ pounds ground beef
1   cup finely chopped sweet white onion, plus 3 onion slices (about ¼-inch thick) for topping
½   cup quick-cooking oats
2   tablespoons whole milk
1   large egg, lightly beaten
1   cup shredded Cheddar cheese
1   tablespoon ketchup
1   tablespoon mayonnaise
1   tablespoon prepared yellow mustard
2   tablespoons sweet pickle relish
¼   teaspoon salt
¼   teaspoon freshly ground pepper
Lettuce leaves for serving
Additional ketchup, mustard, and pickles for serving

Preheat the oven to 350°F. In a large bowl, combine all the ingredients except the onion slices, lettuce leaves, and extra ketchup, mustard, and pickles and mix well. Turn the mixture into a lightly sprayed or oiled 9-by-5-inch loaf pan and gently pat down. Arrange the onion slices on top, keeping them intact. Bake until the loaf is firm and the onions are lightly browned, about 1 hour. Let stand in the pan for 5 to 10 minutes before serving. Remove the loaf from the pan and slice. Line a platter with the lettuce leaves and arrange the meatloaf on top. Serve with ketchup, mustard, and pickles.

FROSTED MEATLOAF

A topping of mashed potatoes highlights this meatloaf, giving it special appeal and delivering meat-and-potatoes satisfaction in each slice. Substitute any fresh fruit you like for the grapes.

Serves 4 to 6

1 pound ground beef
½ pound ground pork sausage
¾ cup quick-cooking oats
1 garlic clove, minced
½ cup tomato juice
1 tablespoon ketchup or chili sauce
1 large egg, lightly beaten
2 or 3 drops Tabasco or other hot-pepper sauce
½ teaspoon salt
¼ teaspoon freshly ground pepper
   Mashed Potato Topping (recipe follows)
   Paprika for sprinkling
   Grapes for garnish

Preheat the oven to 350°F. In a large bowl, combine all the ingredients except the topping, paprika, and grapes and mix well. Turn the mixture into a lightly sprayed or oiled 9-by-5-inch loaf pan and gently pat down. Bake until the loaf is firm and the top is lightly browned, about 1 hour. Remove from the oven and spread the potato mixture on top of the loaf. Sprinkle with paprika. Preheat the broiler, positioning the rack about 6 inches from the heat source. Slip the meatloaf under the broiler and broil until the topping is golden and puffy, about 2 minutes; watch carefully to prevent burning. Let stand in the pan for 5 to 10 minutes before serving. Remove the loaf carefully from the pan and transfer to a platter. Garnish with the grapes.

MASHED POTATO TOPPING

The egg and mayonnaise bind the potatoes together for easier slicing.

2 cups Fluffy Mashed Potatoes (page 91)
1 large egg, lightly beaten
2 tablespoons mayonnaise
2 tablespoons freshly grated Parmesan cheese
½ teaspoon salt

In a medium bowl, mix together all the ingredients. *makes about 2¼ cups*

CHEESY MEATLOAF

This meatloaf is made in a square dish instead of a loaf pan and cut into squares to serve, surprising diners with a rich filling of three kinds of cheese. A layer of tomato slices on top gives it a rustic visual appeal. Serve with Smashed New Potatoes and Cilantro (page 92) for a company dinner.

1   pound ground beef

¾   pound ground pork sausage

¾   cup fine dried bread crumbs

2   large eggs, lightly beaten

2   tablespoons soy sauce

2   tablespoons ketchup

1   teaspoon prepared yellow mustard

1   teaspoon Worcestershire Sauce

½   teaspoon salt

¼   teaspoon freshly ground pepper, plus more to sprinkle on tomatoes

1   cup packed shredded Cheddar cheese

⅓   cup freshly grated Parmesan cheese, divided

¼   cup crumbled blue cheese or Gorgonzola

½   cup chopped green onions, including some tender green tops

1   medium tomato, sliced and drained for topping

2   tablespoons chopped fresh parsley

Preheat the oven to 350°F. In a large bowl, combine all the ingredients except the cheeses, green onions, tomato slices, and parsley, and mix well. Spread half of the meat mixture in a lightly sprayed or oiled 8-by-8-inch glass baking dish or pan.

Layer on the Cheddar cheese, leaving a 1-inch border to help prevent the filling from oozing out. Sprinkle with 3 tablespoons of the Parmesan, all of the blue cheese, and the green onions. Add the remaining meat mixture on top and press firmly around the sides to enclose the cheese and onions. Bake for 50 minutes. Arrange the tomato slices attractively on top, overlapping slightly, if necessary. Sprinkle generously with pepper, the remaining Parmesan cheese, and the parsley. Bake until the tomatoes are lightly browned and the cheese is melted, about 10 minutes longer. Let stand in the pan for 5 to 10 minutes before serving. Cut into squares to serve.

BISTRO MEATLOAF

Serves 4 to 6

Pack a basket with fruit, cheese, and a baguette along with this moist meatloaf and a bottle of your favorite red wine for a picnic at the beach. This meatloaf is good served hot or cold, but chill thoroughly if transporting.

1	pound ground beef
½	pound ground pork sausage
½	cup chopped yellow onion
1	garlic clove, minced
¼	cup chopped fresh parsley
¾	cup fine dried bread crumbs
1	large egg, lightly beaten
¼	cup dry red wine
1	tablespoon Dijon mustard
½	teaspoon dried herbes de Provence
1	teaspoon salt
¼	teaspoon freshly ground pepper
	Cherry tomatoes and parsley sprigs for garnish

Preheat the oven to 350°F.

In a large bowl, combine all the ingredients except the cherry tomatoes and parsley sprigs, and mix well. Turn the mixture into a lightly sprayed or oiled 9-by-5-inch loaf pan and gently pat down. Bake until the loaf is firm and the top is lightly browned, about 1 hour. Let stand in the pan for 5 to 10 minutes before serving. Remove the loaf from the pan and slice to serve. Garnish with the tomatoes and parsley sprigs.

SPINACH-PARMESAN MEATLOAF

The addition of spinach gives extra flavor and body to this meatloaf. *Serves 6*
The spinach also makes an appealing pattern throughout the loaf
when it is sliced. Dijon Mashed Potatoes (page 91) are a good choice
to serve alongside.

1½ pounds ground beef

½ package (5 ounces) frozen
chopped spinach, thawed
and squeezed dry

¼ cup chopped yellow onion

1 garlic clove, minced

2 tablespoons chopped
fresh parsley

½ cup finely crushed saltines
(about 10)

½ cup freshly grated Parmesan
cheese

¼ cup whole milk

¼ teaspoon dried thyme

½ teaspoon salt

¼ teaspoon freshly ground
pepper

Pinch of freshly grated nutmeg

Black olives for garnish

Preheat the oven to 350°F. In a large bowl, combine all the ingredients except the olives and mix well. Turn the mixture into a lightly sprayed or oiled 9-by-5-inch loaf pan and gently pat down. Bake until the loaf is firm and the top is lightly browned, about 1 hour. Let stand in the pan for 5 to 10 minutes before serving. Remove the loaf from the pan and slice to serve. Garnish with the olives.

MEATLOAF WITH *horseradish crumb topping*

A horseradish–bread crumb topping livens up this meatloaf   *Serves 4 to 6*
and adds a zesty flavor. Serve with Garlic Mashed Potatoes
(page 91) and you will have happy diners.

1½ pounds ground beef

½   cup chopped yellow onion

¼   cup chopped fresh parsley

2   garlic cloves, minced

½   cup finely crushed saltines (about 10)

1   large egg, lightly beaten

¼   cup whole milk

3   tablespoons ketchup

1   teaspoon Worcestershire sauce

2   drops Tabasco or other hot-pepper sauce

½   teaspoon salt

¼   teaspoon freshly ground pepper

    Horseradish Crumb Topping (recipe
      follows)

    Parsley or dill sprigs for garnish

Preheat the oven to 350°F. In a large bowl, combine all the ingredients except the topping and garnish, and mix well. Turn the mixture into a lightly sprayed or oiled 9-by-5-inch loaf pan and gently pat down. Bake until the loaf is firm and the top is lightly browned, about 1 hour. Remove from the oven and spread the crumb topping on top of the loaf. Preheat the broiler, positioning the rack about 6 inches from the heat source. Slip the meatloaf under the broiler and broil until the topping is toasted, about 2 minutes; watch carefully to prevent burning. Let stand in the pan for 5 to 10 minutes before serving. Remove the loaf from the pan, transfer to a platter, and garnish.

HORSERADISH CRUMB TOPPING
This is also good on vegetables.

³/4 cup coarse dried bread crumbs

2   tablespoons prepared horseradish sauce

3   tablespoons butter, melted

makes about ¾ cup   In a medium bowl, mix together all the ingredients.

MEATLOAF ON THE GRILL *with spicy barbecue sauce*

Serves 4 to 6 — Meatloaf doesn't have to be reserved for winter menus. Try this unique grilled meatloaf with corn on the cob and Grilled Cheesy Potato Wedges (page 97) for a summer barbecue. You'll need a covered grill. For variety, serve meatloaf sliced in warmed buns, topped with the barbecue sauce.

1   pound ground beef

½   pound ground mild Italian sausage

¼   cup finely chopped green onions, including some tender green tops

½   cup finely chopped red or green bell pepper

¼   cup chopped fresh parsley

2   garlic cloves, minced

1   cup fine dried bread crumbs

1   large egg, lightly beaten

¼   cup whole milk

3   tablespoons ketchup

1   teaspoon Worcestershire sauce

2   or 3 drops Tabasco or other hot-pepper sauce

½   teaspoon salt

¼   teaspoon freshly ground pepper

Spicy Barbecue Sauce (recipe follows), divided

Prepare a fire in a charcoal grill or preheat a gas grill to medium. In a large bowl, combine all the ingredients except the barbecue sauce and mix well. Transfer the mixture to a lightly sprayed or oiled 8-by-8-inch foil pan and shape into a round loaf with a mounded top, leaving ½ inch of space around the edges of the pan. Cover and grill for 30 minutes. Pour 1 cup of the barbecue sauce over the meatloaf and grill until the loaf is firm and the sauce is bubbly, about 30 minutes longer. Remove from the grill and let stand for 5 to 10 minutes before serving. Remove the loaf from the pan, transfer to a platter, and slice to serve. Serve the remaining sauce in a small pitcher.

SPICY BARBECUE SAUCE

This all-purpose barbecue sauce is great for hamburgers, ribs, chicken, and beef or pork sandwiches, or as a sauce with meatballs.

¾ cup ketchup

¼ cup chili sauce

1 tablespoon cider vinegar

1 cup water

1 tablespoon Worcestershire sauce

1 tablespoon honey

1 teaspoon fresh lemon juice

½ teaspoon chili powder

¼ teaspoon garlic powder

¼ teaspoon salt

In a small saucepan over medium heat, combine all the ingredients and simmer until the flavors are blended, 5 to 10 minutes.

makes about 2 cups

GLAZED MEATLOAF *with bacon strips*

A topping of a sweet, spicy glaze and crispy bacon slices sets this meatloaf apart. Serve with Steamed New Potatoes with Fresh Basil (page 93) for a summer meal that pairs complementary flavors with the garden's fresh bounty.

Serves 4 to 6

1   pound ground beef
½   pound ground pork sausage
½   cup chopped yellow onion
½   cup chopped red bell pepper
½   cup finely crushed saltines
      (about 10)
1   large egg, lightly beaten
½   cup whole milk
¼   cup freshly grated
      Parmesan cheese
½   teaspoon salt
¼   teaspoon freshly ground
      pepper
      Chili Glaze (recipe follows)
3   bacon strips, precooked
      for 1 minute (see Note)
      Parsley sprigs for garnish

Preheat the oven to 350°F. In a large bowl, combine all the ingredients except the glaze, bacon, and parsley and mix well. Turn the mixture into a lightly sprayed or oiled 9-by-5-inch loaf pan and gently pat down. Spread the glaze on top of the loaf and arrange the bacon strips neatly to cover. Bake until the loaf is firm and the bacon is crisp, about 1 hour. Let stand in the pan for 5 to 10 minutes before serving. Remove the loaf from the pan and transfer to a platter. Garnish with the parsley sprigs.

NOTE: *To slightly precook the bacon, place the strips on a paper plate lined with a paper towel and place another paper towel on top. Microwave for about 1 minute to remove excess fat.*

CHILI GLAZE
This glaze adds flavor and appeal.

1   tablespoon brown sugar
½   cup red chili sauce
½   teaspoon chili powder
1   teaspoon Worcestershire sauce

In a small bowl, mix together all the ingredients.

makes about ½ cup

MEATLOAF WITH *bell pepper sauté*

Serves 6

This meatloaf smothered with a mixed sauté of bell peppers and onion makes a colorful presentation. For a complementary side dish with flavor to match, serve with Garlic Mashed Potatoes (page 91).

1   pound ground beef

½   pound ground pork sausage

½   cup chopped yellow onion

½   cup chopped green bell pepper

¾   cup finely crushed saltines (about 15)

½   cup whole milk

1   large egg, lightly beaten

¼   cup freshly grated Parmesan cheese

1   teaspoon salt

¼   teaspoon freshly ground pepper

Bell Pepper Sauté (recipe follows) for serving

Preheat the oven to 350°F. In a large bowl, combine all the ingredients except the Bell Pepper Sauté and mix well. Turn the mixture into a lightly sprayed or oiled 9-by-5-inch loaf pan and gently pat down. Bake until the loaf is firm and the top is lightly browned, about 1 hour. Let stand in the pan for 5 to 10 minutes before serving. Remove the loaf from the pan and transfer to a platter. Spread the sautéed peppers over the top and serve immediately.

BELL PEPPER SAUTÉ

This mixture of sautéed red, green, and yellow bell peppers makes an appealing accompaniment for almost any meat.

2   to 3 tablespoons olive oil

2   garlic cloves, chopped

1   red bell pepper, seeded and sliced lengthwise into ⅜-inch strips

BEEF AND PORTOBELLO MEATLOAF

Portobello mushrooms are large, mature cremini mushrooms. They are often used in place of hamburger patties in buns for a grilled sandwich. In this meatloaf, the mushroom imparts a subtle, earthy flavor and keeps the meatloaf moist.

1   green bell pepper, seeded and sliced lengthwise into ⅜-inch strips

1   yellow bell pepper, seeded and sliced lengthwise into ⅜-inch strips

1   yellow onion, sliced and separated into rings

1   tablespoon chopped fresh basil or 1 teaspoon dried basil

½   teaspoon salt

¼   teaspoon freshly ground pepper

In a large sauté pan over medium heat, warm 2 tablespoons of the olive oil. Add the garlic, bell peppers, and onion and sauté until tender-crisp, about 10 minutes. Add more oil if necessary to prevent sticking. Add the basil, salt, and pepper and sauté until the flavors are blended, 2 to 3 minutes longer.

makes about 3 cups

1   tablespoon butter

1   portobello mushroom, about 4 ounces, stem removed and gills scraped and discarded, chopped

½   cup chopped yellow onion

½   cup finely chopped green bell pepper

2   garlic cloves, minced

1   pound ground beef

½   pound ground veal

1   cup coarse dried bread crumbs

¼   cup beef broth

1   large egg, lightly beaten

1   tablespoon chopped fresh parsley

½   cup ketchup, divided

1   tablespoon Worcestershire sauce

1   or 2 drops Tabasco sauce

¼   teaspoon dried basil

¼   teaspoon dried oregano

¾   teaspoon salt

¼   teaspoon freshly ground pepper

Parsley sprigs for garnish

continued

BEEF AND PORTOBELLO MEATLOAF

continued

Preheat the oven to 350°F. In a small skillet over medium heat, melt the butter. Add the mushroom, onion, bell pepper, and garlic and sauté until tender, about 5 minutes. Transfer to a large bowl, add the remaining ingredients except ¼ cup of the ketchup and the parsley sprigs, and mix well. Turn the mixture into a lightly sprayed or oiled 9-by-5-inch loaf pan and gently pat down. Spread the reserved ketchup on top of the loaf. Bake until the loaf is firm and the top is lightly browned, about 1 hour. Let stand in the pan for 5 to 10 minutes before serving. Remove the loaf from the pan and slice to serve. Garnish with the parsley sprigs.

Serves 6

REUBEN MEATLOAF

Serves 4 *You'll find all your favorite ingredients of the classic Reuben sandwich in this loaf topped with sauerkraut and cheese. Serve with dark rye bread and cold beer. Use the leftover meatloaf in sandwiches (see page 46) for a delicious deli-style treat the next day.*

1   pound cooked corned beef, cut into chunks and ground in a food processor
½   pound ground beef
½   cup dried rye or pumpernickel bread crumbs
1   large egg, lightly beaten
⅓   cup Quick Thousand Island Dressing (page 46)
½   teaspoon salt
¼   teaspoon freshly ground pepper
1   jar (16 ounces) sauerkraut, drained, divided for topping on loaf and for sandwiches
3   large slices Swiss cheese
    Parsley sprigs for garnish

continued

Preheat the oven to 350°F. In a large bowl, combine all the ingredients except the sauerkraut, cheese, and parsley and mix well. Turn the mixture into a lightly sprayed or oiled 9-by-5-inch loaf pan and gently pat down. Bake for 45 minutes. Spread 1 cup of the sauerkraut on top of the loaf and cover with the cheese slices. Bake until the sauerkraut is hot and the cheese is melted, about 15 minutes longer. Let stand for 5 to 10 minutes before serving. Remove the loaf from the pan and slice to serve. Garnish with the parsley sprigs.

QUICK THOUSAND ISLAND DRESSING

Use the remaining dressing for next-day reuben sandwiches. This dressing is also good with fresh crab and other seafood.

1   cup mayonnaise

¼   cup red chili sauce

1   teaspoon Worcestershire sauce

2   teaspoons sweet pickle relish

¼   teaspoon salt

In a medium bowl, whisk together all the ingredients. Cover and refrigerate until ready to use.

makes about 1¼ cups

NEXT–DAY
REUBEN SANDWICHES

These toasted sandwiches make a hearty meal. They can be made either in a sandwich-maker or in a skillet on top of the stove.

4   slices dark bread such as
     pumpernickel or rye
     Quick Thousand Island Dressing (at left)

2   ⅜-inch slices of leftover REUBEN MEAT-
     LOAF cut to fit the bread

2   slices Swiss cheese
     Remaining sauerkraut
     Butter for spreading on the top of the
     bread slices and for the sandwich-maker

Preheat a sandwich-maker. Spread one side of each slice of bread with dressing. Put a meatloaf slice on 2 of the bread slices and top each with a slice of Swiss cheese. Pile on sauerkraut to taste and top with the remaining bread slices. Butter the top of the top slices and butter the bottom of the sandwich-maker. Add the sandwiches, lower the lid and toast until lightly browned, about 5 minutes total.

makes 2 sandwiches

BEEF AND **HAM** MEATLOAF

The addition of ham gives a light, smoky flavor to this popular meatloaf. Serve with Twice-Baked Potatoes (page 94) or plain baked potatoes for a satisfying family-night meal.

Serves 4 to 6

¾ pound ground beef
¾ pound ground cooked ham
   (prepared by the butcher)
     or 1 thick slice ham (¾ pound),
     cut into cubes and ground
     in a food processor
¾ cup finely crushed saltines
     (about 15)
½ cup whole milk
2 large eggs, lightly beaten
1 tablespoon Dijon mustard
3 tablespoons chopped fresh
     parsley
½ teaspoon salt
¼ teaspoon freshly ground pepper
   Parsley sprigs for garnish
   Additional Dijon mustard for
     serving

Preheat the oven to 350°F. In a large bowl, combine all the ingredients except the parsley sprigs and additional mustard and mix well. Turn the mixture into a lightly sprayed or oiled 9-by-5-inch loaf pan and gently pat down. Bake until the loaf is firm and the top is lightly browned, about 1 hour. Let stand in the pan for 5 to 10 minutes before serving. Remove the loaf from the pan and slice to serve. Garnish with the parsley sprigs and serve with additional mustard.

HAM AND **PORK** MEATLOAF *with honey-mustard sauce*

Serves 6 A combination of ground ham and pork makes a savory loaf to serve as a main course for a company dinner or for a luncheon. It is dressed up with a spicy sauce and garnished with pineapple rings. *Bourbon Sweet Potatoes with Pecans (page 99)* make a festive side dish. Use the leftover sauce on sandwiches the next day.

HONEY-MUSTARD SAUCE

1 tablespoon brown sugar

1 teaspoon cider vinegar

½ teaspoon dried dill

3 tablespoons Dijon mustard

1 tablespoon prepared yellow mustard

¼ cup sour cream

1 tablespoon honey

In a small bowl, stir together the brown sugar and vinegar until the sugar is dissolved. Add the remaining ingredients and whisk until smooth. Serve at room temperature.

makes about ¾ cup

¾ pound ground cooked ham prepared by the butcher or one thick ham slice (¾ pound), cut into cubes and ground in a food processor

¾ pound ground pork

½ cup diced yellow onion

¾ cup finely crushed saltines (about 15)

½ cup whole milk

1 large egg, lightly beaten

2 teaspoons Dijon mustard

¼ teaspoon dried thyme

1 teaspoon dry mustard

½ teaspoon salt

¼ teaspoon freshly ground pepper

1 can (4 ounces) pineapple slices, drained

Honey-Mustard Sauce (recipe at left) for serving

Preheat the oven to 350°F. In a large bowl, combine all the ingredients except the pineapple slices and sauce and mix well. Turn the mixture into a lightly sprayed or oiled 8-by-8-inch glass baking dish and shape into a square, leaving ½ inch of space around the edges of the dish. Bake until the loaf is firm and the top is lightly browned, about 50 minutes. Pour off any accumulated fat. Lay the pineapple slices attractively on top of the loaf and bake until the pineapple is lightly browned, about 10 minutes longer. Let stand in the pan for 5 to 10 minutes before serving. Remove the loaf from the pan and transfer to a platter. Serve with the Honey-Mustard Sauce.

BLOODY MARY MEATLOAF

Gather around the table and have some fun with this spirited meatloaf. The addition of vodka makes for good conversation, but you can leave it out or drink it if you wish.

Serves 4 to 6

½ pound ground beef

½ pound ground veal

½ pound ground pork

½ cup diced yellow onion

¼ cup diced celery

¼ cup chopped parsley

¾ cup fine dried bread crumbs

½ cup Bloody Mary mix or spicy vegetable juice (such as V8)

1 large egg, lightly beaten

2 to 3 tablespoons vodka (optional)

1 teaspoon Worcestershire sauce

2 or 3 drops Tabasco or other hot-pepper sauce

1 teaspoon chili powder

½ teaspoon celery seed

½ teaspoon salt

¼ teaspoon freshly ground pepper

   Bloody Mary Sauce (recipe follows)

   Celery sticks for garnish

1 jar (12 ounces) pickled asparagus spears or pickled beans, drained, for garnish (optional)

Preheat the oven to 350°F. In a large bowl, combine all the ingredients except the Bloody Mary Sauce and garnishes, and mix well. Divide the mixture equally into 4 individual round loaves. Place into a lightly sprayed or oiled 8-by-8-inch glass baking dish. Bake until the loaves are firm and the top is lightly browned, about 40 minutes. Let stand 5 to 10 minutes. To serve, pour some of the warm Bloody Mary Sauce on 4 individual plates. Place the meatloaves on top of the sauce and pour some of the sauce over. Add garnishes, if using.

BLOODY MARY SAUCE

1 can (8 ounces) tomato sauce

1 or 2 tablespoons vodka

1 teaspoon Worcestershire sauce

1 teaspoon prepared horseradish sauce

2 or 3 drops Tabasco sauce or other hot-pepper sauce

¼ teaspoon salt

   Freshly ground pepper

In a small saucepan over medium heat, mix together all the ingredients. Cook until flavors are blended, about 5 minutes.

makes about 1 cup

breakfast MEATLOAF **BENEDICT**

Serves 4 to 6 Not all meatloaf is for dinner. You will impress your overnight or brunch guests with this intriguing takeoff on eggs Benedict. A poached egg is added to sausage loaf slices and topped with Hollandaise sauce for a special treat. Serve with hash browns (page 98) and additional toasted English muffins. You'll probably have meatloaf left over for a late-night snack!

NOTE: An egg poacher is a pan designed specifically to poach eggs perfectly every time, and is a worthwhile investment for making this often frustrating process as simple as it should be. The eggs are cooked in individual cups over simmering water, covered, forming each into a neat, uniformly round shape. Follow the manufacturer's simple directions. If you don't have an egg poacher, use a pan of simmering water as described on the next page. The eggs will look a bit more uneven around the edges and some of the white may be lost.

1½ pounds ground pork sausage
¾ cup quick-cooking oats
½ cup tomato juice
1   large egg, lightly beaten
½ teaspoon salt
¼ teaspoon freshly ground pepper
2   or 3 English muffins, split and toasted
4   to 6 poached eggs (see Notes) Hollandaise Sauce (recipe follows) for serving

Preheat the oven to 350°F. In a large bowl, combine all the ingredients except the muffins, poached eggs, and Hollandaise Sauce and mix well. Turn the mixture into a lightly sprayed or oiled 9-by-5-inch loaf pan and gently pat down. Bake until the loaf is firm and the top is lightly browned, about 1 hour. Let stand in the pan for 5 to 10 minutes before serving. Remove the loaf from the pan and slice. Divide the muffin halves among individual plates. Place a slice of meatloaf on each English muffin half. Add a poached egg to each and top with Hollandaise Sauce.

HOLLANDAISE SAUCE

This lemony hollandaise sauce is safe from salmonella because the egg yolks are cooked. It is also wonderful on asparagus and other vegetables.

4   egg yolks

3   tablespoons fresh lemon juice

1   tablespoon water

¼   teaspoon salt

    Dash of cayenne pepper

1   cup (2 sticks) unsalted butter (no substitute), melted

In a small, heavy saucepan over medium-low heat, combine the egg yolks, lemon juice, water, salt, and cayenne pepper. Whisk constantly until the mixture bubbles and begins to thicken, 2 to 3 minutes. Using a heatproof spatula, transfer the mixture to a blender. With the motor running, add the melted butter in a slow, steady stream and blend until all the butter is used and the sauce is thickened, about 30 seconds. Use immediately, or keep the remaining sauce warm in a pan over warm water until ready to use.

makes about 1½ cups

NOTE: **To poach eggs** in a deep skillet or saucepan, bring 1½ inches of water to a gentle boil over medium-high heat. Reduce the heat to low and stir in 1 teaspoon white vinegar and 1 teaspoon salt. Break an egg into a small bowl or cup and slip it into the water. Repeat, adding 1 to 3 eggs clockwise; do not crowd the pan.

Cover and simmer for 3 to 4 minutes, or to desired doneness. Do not allow the water to boil. Remove the eggs with a slotted spoon in the order they were added to the pan and blot the bottoms with a paper towel. Trim the edges for a neat, even look with kitchen scissors, if desired.

REUNION MEATLOAF

Serves 4 to 6 *Greek and Italian flavors come together in this smooth, fine-textured meatloaf served with a refreshing cucumber sauce. I took it to our family reunion and it disappeared fast!*

1   pound ground lamb
½   pound ground veal or turkey
½   cup finely chopped yellow
        onion
3   garlic cloves, minced
¾   cup dried bread crumbs
1   large egg, lightly beaten
½   cup plain nonfat yogurt
        or sour cream
¾   cup shredded mozzarella
        cheese
2   tablespoons chopped fresh
        mint leaves
½   teaspoon dried oregano
½   teaspoon salt
¼   teaspoon freshly ground
        pepper
      Sliced tomatoes, cucumbers,
        and fresh mint leaves for
        garnish
      Tzatziki (page 76) for serving

In a large bowl, combine all the ingredients except the tomatoes, cucumbers, whole mint leaves, and Tzatziki and mix well. Turn the mixture into a lightly sprayed or oiled 9-by-5-inch loaf pan and gently pat down. Bake until the loaf is firm and the top is lightly browned, about 1 hour. Let stand in the pan for 5 to 10 minutes before serving. Remove the loaf from the pan and slice to serve. Garnish with the tomato and cucumber slices and mint leaves. Serve with the Tzatziki.

ROLLED **DELI** MEATLOAF

The addition of a ham, salami, and cheese stuffing elevates this meatloaf to company fare. When sliced, it reveals an impressive pinwheel pattern. It may sound complicated, but it is actually easy to make and fun to serve. I serve cold slices of this loaf to friends along with corn on the cob, sliced cucumbers, and a wedge of lettuce with blue cheese dressing for a light summer supper on the deck.

2	pounds ground beef
½	cup chopped red onion
2	garlic cloves, minced
1	cup coarse dried sourdough bread crumbs
½	cup tomato juice
2	large eggs, lightly beaten
1	tablespoon prepared creamy horseradish sauce
½	teaspoon salt
¼	teaspoon freshly ground pepper
4	large, thin deli ham slices
8	thin salami slices
6	thin Swiss cheese slices
	Parsley sprigs for garnish
	Whole-grain mustard for serving

Serves 8 to 10

Preheat the oven to 350°F. In a large bowl, combine all the ingredients except the ham, salami, cheese, parsley, and mustard. On a piece of waxed paper, shape the mixture into an 11-by-14-inch rectangle about ½ inch thick. Arrange the meat and cheese slices on top of the mixture, leaving a ½-inch border around the edges. Starting from the short end, roll the assembled meat into a log, using the waxed paper to lift. Press the ends and seam together to seal. Place the rolled loaf, seam-side down, in a lightly sprayed or oiled 9-by-13-inch glass baking dish and remove the waxed paper. Bake until the loaf is firm and the top is lightly browned, about 1 hour and 10 minutes. Let stand in the dish for 5 to 10 minutes before serving. Slice and transfer to a platter and garnish with the parsley. Serve with the mustard.

MICROWAVE MEATLOAF

Serves 4 In just 12 minutes, you can have a meatloaf ready for the dinner table. While the meatloaf rests, microwave some baking potatoes, about 7 to 8 minutes, to accompany your meal.

1   pound ground beef
½   cup finely chopped yellow
    onion
½   cup quick-cooking oats
1   egg, lightly beaten
¼   cup whole milk
2   tablespoons ketchup
1   tablespoon prepared mustard
½   teaspoon salt
¼   teaspoon freshly ground
    pepper
    Sweet Glaze (recipe follows)

In a medium bowl, mix together all the ingredients except the glaze. In a lightly sprayed or oiled 9-inch glass pie plate, form the meatloaf around a lightly sprayed or oiled 3-inch ramekin dish or custard cup placed upside down in the center of the pie plate. Cook in the microwave on high for 10 minutes. Spread on the glaze and cook on high for 2 minutes longer. Let stand in the pie plate for 5 minutes before serving. Serve the loaf from the pie plate.

SWEET GLAZE

1   tablespoon brown sugar
½   cup ketchup
1   teaspoon prepared yellow
    mustard
¼   teaspoon dried thyme

In a small bowl, mix together all the ingredients.
makes about ½ cup

PIZZA MEATLOAF

This great loaf has all the elements of a popular pizza. Make it when your kids have friends over for dinner and you'll have a hit. Consider making two if you are feeding a crowd.

Serves 6

1½ pounds Italian pork sausage
½ cup chopped green bell pepper
½ cup chopped yellow onion
¾ cup dried bread crumbs
1 large egg, lightly beaten
¼ teaspoon dried oregano
¼ teaspoon salt
¼ teaspoon freshly ground pepper
1 jar (7 ounces) pizza sauce, divided
½ cup sliced mushrooms
18 to 20 pepperoni slices
¾ cup shredded Cheddar cheese

Preheat the oven to 350°F. In a large bowl, combine all the ingredients except half of the pizza sauce, the mushrooms, the pepperoni, and the cheese and mix well. Turn the mixture into a lightly sprayed or oiled 9-by-5-inch loaf pan and gently pat down. Bake for 30 minutes. Spread the reserved pizza sauce on top of the loaf and arrange the mushrooms and pepperoni slices on the sauce, slightly overlapping. Sprinkle the cheese over. Bake until the loaf is firm and the sauce is bubbly, about 30 minutes longer. Let stand in the pan for 5 to 10 minutes before serving. Remove the loaf from the pan and slice to serve.

SAUSAGE-CLAM MEATLOAF

Serves 6

You may not detect the clams in this meatloaf, but they add extra liquid, texture, and a subtle flavor. Serve this delicious meatloaf hot as a main course, cold in sandwiches, or as an hors d'oeuvre on baguette slices.

1   **pound ground pork sausage (see Note)**

½   **cup finely chopped yellow onion**

1   **cup finely crushed saltines (about 20)**

1   **large egg, lightly beaten**

1   **can (6 ½ ounces) chopped clams with liquid**

1   **tablespoon Dijon mustard**

½   **teaspoon salt**

¼   **teaspoon freshly ground pepper**

Dijon Mayonnaise (recipe at left) for serving

Preheat the oven to 350°F. In a large bowl, combine all the ingredients except the mayonnaise and mix well. Turn the mixture into a lightly sprayed or oiled 9-by-5-inch loaf pan and gently pat down. Bake until the loaf is firm and the top is lightly browned, about 1 hour. Let stand in the pan for 5 to 10 minutes before serving. Remove the loaf from the pan, slice, and serve with the Dijon Mayonnaise.

NOTE: *If serving the meatloaf for an hors d'oeuvre, grind the sausage again in the food processor for a finer, pâté-like texture.*

DIJON MAYONNAISE

¼   *cup mayonnaise*

¼   *cup plain nonfat yogurt*

2   *tablespoons Dijon mustard*

1   *teaspoon fresh lemon juice*

In a small bowl, stir together all the ingredients until well blended. Serve at room temperature.

makes about ½ cup

MEATLOAF WITH **KIELBASA**

This creative combination of mild turkey and spicy kielbasa   *Serves 6*
sausage gives a good balance of contrasting flavors and
texture. Kielbasa is made from pork and beef and is highly
seasoned. Serve Steamed New Potatoes with Fresh Basil
(page 93) and applesauce as accompaniments.

1 pound ground turkey

½ pound kielbasa, sliced and
   coarsely chopped in a food
   processor

½ cup finely crushed saltines
   (about 10)

½ cup diced yellow onion

1 garlic clove, minced

3 ounces mushrooms, chopped

½ cup finely chopped red bell
   pepper

1 large egg, lightly beaten

¼ cup whole milk

3 tablespoons ketchup

2 teaspoons Worcestershire
   sauce

½ teaspoon salt

¼ teaspoon freshly ground
   pepper

Preheat the oven to 350°F. In a large bowl, combine all the ingredients and mix well. Turn the mixture into a lightly sprayed or oiled 9-by-5-inch loaf pan and gently pat down. Bake until the loaf is firm and the top is lightly browned, about 1 hour. Let stand in the pan for 5 to 10 minutes before serving. Remove the loaf from the pan and slice to serve.

CAJUN MEATLOAF

Andouille sausage makes a spicy addition to this loaf. A specialty of Cajun cooking, it is a highly seasoned, heavily smoked sausage made from pork. Add Pecan Rice (page 102) and a cooling glass of iced tea to the menu.

1	pound ground beef
½	pound andouille sausage, casings removed, crumbled
½	cup chopped yellow onion
½	cup chopped green bell pepper
2	garlic cloves, minced
¾	cup dried bread crumbs
½	cup whole milk
1	large egg, lightly beaten
¼	cup ketchup
1	tablespoon Worcestershire sauce
½	teaspoon Tabasco or other hot-pepper sauce
½	teaspoon ground cumin
½	teaspoon paprika

Preheat the oven to 350°F. In a large bowl, combine all the ingredients and mix well. Turn the mixture into a lightly sprayed or oiled 9-by-5-inch loaf pan and gently pat down. Bake until the loaf is firm and the top is lightly browned, about 1 hour. Let stand in the pan for 5 to 10 minutes before serving. Remove the loaf from the pan and slice to serve.

TEX-MEX MEATLOAF

Serves 4 to 6 This meatloaf combines the popular flavors of Tex-Mex
cooking. Cilantro, a fresh herb used extensively in Mexican
and Asian cooking, is similar to parsley but more pungent.
It has bright green leaves and stems with a fresh, lively taste.

1   pound ground beef
½   pound ground pork sausage
½   cup finely chopped yellow
      onion
½   cup finely chopped red or
      green bell pepper
¼   cup chopped fresh cilantro
2   garlic cloves, minced
¾   cup dried bread crumbs
1   large egg, lightly beaten
¼   cup red chili sauce
1   teaspoon Worcestershire
      sauce
½   teaspoon ground cumin
½   teaspoon ground oregano
½   teaspoon chili powder
½   teaspoon salt
¼   teaspoon freshly ground
      pepper
     Cilantro sprigs for garnish

Preheat the oven to 350°F.
In a large bowl, combine all
the ingredients except the
cilantro sprigs and mix well.
Turn the mixture into a lightly
sprayed or oiled 9-by-5-inch
loaf pan and gently pat down.
Bake until the loaf is firm and
the top is lightly browned,
about 1 hour. Let stand in the
pan for 5 to 10 minutes before
serving. Remove the loaf from
the pan and slice to serve.
Garnish with the cilantro
sprigs.

SOUTHWEST MEATLOAF

Serves 4 to 6

This festive meatloaf with chiles has a lot of kick and flavor. When the loaf is sliced, a colorful pattern of green and red peppers studded throughout the loaf is revealed. Serve with Mexican-Style Twice-Baked Potatoes (page 94), warm tortillas, sour cream, and additional salsa.

1   pound ground beef
½   pound ground pork sausage
½   cup chopped yellow onion
½   cup chopped red bell pepper
½   cup chopped green bell pepper
2   garlic cloves, minced
½   cup quick-cooking oats
1   can (4 ounces) diced green chiles, drained
½   cup tomato juice
1   large egg, lightly beaten
1   teaspoon chili powder
½   teaspoon ground cumin
½   teaspoon dried oregano
½   teaspoon salt
¼   teaspoon freshly ground pepper
    Fresh Tomato Salsa (recipe follows) or purchased salsa for serving
    Sour cream for serving

Preheat the oven to 350°F.

In a large bowl, combine all the ingredients except the salsa and sour cream and mix well. Turn the mixture into a lightly sprayed or oiled 9-by-5-inch loaf pan and gently pat down. Bake until the loaf is firm and the top is lightly browned, about 1 hour. Let stand in the pan for 5 to 10 minutes before serving. Remove the loaf from the pan and slice to serve. Serve with the salsa and sour cream.

FRESH TOMATO SALSA

This popular salsa is best served the day it is made, but should be made several hours ahead to allow the flavors to blend.

4 medium tomatoes, seeded, chopped, and drained

½ cup diced green bell pepper

½ cup diced white onion

1 jalapeño chile, seeded and finely chopped (see Note)

2 garlic cloves, minced

Juice of 1 small lime

1 tablespoon olive oil

¼ cup chopped fresh cilantro or parsley

1 tablespoon chopped fresh oregano or 1 teaspoon dried oregano

½ teaspoon salt

¼ teaspoon freshly ground pepper

In a medium bowl, stir together all the ingredients. Cover and let stand at room temperature for at least 1 hour. Drain, if necessary, before using.

makes about 3½ cups

NOTE: **When handling chiles,** wear latex gloves or hold the chiles under running cold water to protect against oils that may cause burning to the skin. Keep your fingers away from your face and eyes, and wash your hands with warm soapy water immediately after handling.

MEXICAN MEATLOAF *with corn and chipotle mayonnaise*

Serves 4 to 6 The addition of corn gives extra texture and a new taste to this Mexican-inspired meatloaf. If you like it hot, serve with a dollop of Chipotle Mayonnaise on top. Chipotle chiles are dried, smoked jalapeños, typically canned in adobo sauce. They have a smoky, sweet flavor and are very hot. Serve with iced tea or cold beer.

CHIPOTLE MAYONNAISE

This sauce is also good on corn on the cob and other vegetables.

½ cup mayonnaise

1 garlic clove, minced

1 canned chipotle chile pepper in adobo sauce, minced

1 teaspoon fresh lime juice

2 tablespoons chopped fresh cilantro

In a small bowl, mix together all the ingredients.

makes about ½ cup

1 pound ground beef
½ pound ground pork sausage
1 cup chopped yellow onion
½ cup finely chopped green bell pepper
2 garlic cloves, minced
1 cup fresh or thawed frozen corn kernels
½ cup coarse dried bread crumbs
3 tablespoons red chili sauce
1 large egg, lightly beaten
½ teaspoon ground cumin
½ teaspoon chili powder
½ teaspoon salt
Chipotle Mayonnaise (recipe at left) for serving
Cilantro sprigs for garnish

Preheat the oven to 350°F. In a large bowl, combine all the ingredients except the mayonnaise and cilantro sprigs and mix well. Turn the mixture into a lightly sprayed or oiled 9-by-5-inch loaf pan and gently pat down. Bake until the loaf is firm and the top is lightly browned, about 1 hour. Let stand in the pan for 5 to 10 minutes before serving. Remove the loaf from the pan and slice to serve. Garnish with the cilantro sprigs and serve with the Chipotle Mayonnaise.

MEXICAN MEATLOAF *with fresh tomato salsa*

This Mexican spiced meatloaf is a hit the first time around and again   *Serves 6*

the next day, sliced and served in sandwiches. In fact, the flavors develop more the next day. Serve with Red and Green Rice (page 100) and additional salsa, along with hot chocolate for a regional touch.

1½   **pounds ground beef**

½   **cup coarsely crushed tortilla chips**

½   **cup chopped white onion**

1   **garlic clove, minced**

2   **tablespoons chopped fresh parsley**

1½ **cups Fresh Tomato Salsa (page 63) or purchased salsa, divided**

1   **large egg, lightly beaten**

½   **teaspoon dried oregano**

¼   **teaspoon ground cumin**

½   **teaspoon salt**

¼   **teaspoon freshly ground pepper**

    Parsley sprigs for garnish

Preheat the oven to 350°F.
In a large bowl, combine all the ingredients except ¾ cup of the salsa and the parsley sprigs, and mix well. Turn the mixture into a lightly sprayed or oiled 9-by-5-inch loaf pan and gently pat down. Bake for 50 minutes. Pour off any accumulated fat. Spread the reserved ¾ cup salsa on top of the loaf and bake until the loaf is firm and the salsa is warmed, about 10 minutes longer. Let stand in the pan for 5 to 10 minutes before serving. Remove the loaf from the pan and slice to serve. Garnish with the parsley sprigs.

SPANISH MEATLOAF

Serves 4 to 6

A mixture of ground pork and chorizo gives this meatloaf spicy bursts of flavor. Chorizo is a highly seasoned ground pork sausage used in Spanish and Mexican cooking. The casing is removed before cooking. Serve with baked sweet potatoes.

1½ pounds ground pork

4 ounces chorizo, casings removed, crumbled

½ cup chopped red bell pepper

½ cup chopped yellow onion

½ cup quick-cooking oats

½ cup spicy vegetable juice (such as V8)

1 large egg, lightly beaten

2 to 3 tablespoons finely chopped fresh cilantro

½ teaspoon paprika

½ teaspoon salt

¼ teaspoon freshly ground pepper

Preheat the oven to 350°F. In a large bowl, combine all the ingredients and mix well. Turn the mixture into a lightly sprayed or oiled cast-iron skillet or 9-inch round baking dish and shape into a round loaf with a mounded top, leaving ½ inch of space around the edges of the pan. Bake until the loaf is firm and the top is lightly browned, about 1 hour. Let stand in the pan for 5 to 10 minutes before serving. Remove the loaf from the pan and slice to serve.

TUSCAN MEATLOAF

A class I took on Tuscan cooking was the inspiration for this flavorful meatloaf. Pancetta is an Italian bacon cured with salt and spices, but not smoked. It imparts a slightly salty flavor to the meatloaf as it bakes. Sip a glass of Chianti as you enjoy this savory meatloaf and dream you are under the Tuscan sky.

Serves 4 to 6

¾ pound ground lamb
¾ pound ground pork
½ cup chopped yellow onion
¾ cup dried bread crumbs
½ cup tomato purée
½ cup crumbled Gorgonzola cheese
1 large egg, lightly beaten
1 tablespoon chopped fresh sage
  or ½ teaspoon dried sage
½ teaspoon dried rosemary
½ teaspoon salt
¼ teaspoon freshly ground pepper
4 pancetta slices
Fresh sage leaves for garnish

In a large bowl, combine all the ingredients except the pancetta and sage leaves and mix well. Turn the mixture into a lightly sprayed or oiled 9-by-5-inch loaf pan and gently pat down. Arrange the pancetta neatly on top of the loaf to cover, slightly overlapping. Bake for 30 minutes, then turn the pancetta. Bake until the loaf is firm and the pancetta is browned and crisp, about 30 minutes longer. Let stand in the pan for 5 to 10 minutes before serving. Remove the loaf from the pan and transfer to a platter. Garnish with the sage leaves.

ITALIAN MEATLOAF

This Italian-inspired meatloaf is flavored with lots of herbs and two cheeses. It has a firm texture and makes excellent cold sandwiches on crusty bread.

Serves 6

1 pound ground beef

½ pound ground mild Italian sausage

½ cup chopped yellow onion

½ cup chopped red or green bell pepper

1 garlic clove, minced

½ cup coarse dried sourdough bread crumbs (see page 13)

2 tablespoons dry red wine (optional)

1 large egg, lightly beaten

1 teaspoon Worcestershire sauce

2 tablespoons chopped fresh parsley

½ teaspoon dried basil

½ teaspoon dried oregano

½ teaspoon salt

¼ teaspoon freshly ground pepper

2 tablespoons freshly grated Parmesan cheese

1 can (8 ounces) tomato sauce, divided

1 cup grated mozzarella cheese

Preheat the oven to 350°F. In a large bowl, combine all the ingredients except ½ cup of the tomato sauce and the mozzarella and mix well. Turn the mixture into a lightly sprayed or oiled 9-by-5-inch loaf pan and gently pat down. Bake for 45 minutes. Spread the remaining tomato sauce on the top of the loaf and sprinkle with mozzarella. Bake until the cheese melts and the sauce is warmed, about 10 minutes longer. Let stand in the pan for 5 to 10 minutes before serving. Remove the loaf from the pan and slice to serve.

MEATLOAF

Serves 4 This fine-textured, lemon-scented loaf can be the centerpiece of a company dinner. Veal is very tender and is considered a delicacy. It is sometimes hard to find ground, but your butcher should be happy to prepare it for you. Here, the ground veal is made into a meatloaf with mushrooms and flavors of the famous Italian dish veal piccata. Serve with a fine white wine and ciabatta bread.

1	pound ground veal
2	shallots, finely chopped
4	ounces mushrooms, chopped
¾	cup fine dried bread crumbs
½	cup light sour cream
1	tablespoon fresh lemon juice
1	large egg, lightly beaten
1	tablespoon capers, drained
2	tablespoons chopped fresh parsley
½	teaspoon salt
¼	teaspoon freshly ground pepper
½	lemon sliced
	Parsley sprigs for garnish

Preheat the oven to 350°F. In a large bowl, combine all the ingredients except the lemon slices and parsley sprigs and mix well. Turn the mixture into a lightly sprayed or oiled 9-by-5-inch loaf pan and gently pat down. Bake for 45 minutes. Arrange the lemon slices on top and bake until the loaf is firm and the lemon slices are warm and juicy, about 15 minutes longer. Let stand in the pan for 5 to 10 minutes before serving. Remove the loaf from the pan and slice to serve. Garnish with the parsley sprigs.

MEDITERRANEAN MEATLOAF *with tomato-caper sauce*

Lentils add body and texture to this meatloaf of turkey and lamb seasoned   *Serves 6*
with herbs and spices. Present this loaf on a platter with a flavorful
tomato sauce poured over the top and garnished with mint leaves. Serve
with steamed artichokes to match the Mediterranean theme.

1   pound ground turkey

¾ pound ground lamb

½ cup chopped yellow onion

1   small carrot, peeled and grated

2   garlic cloves, minced

1   cup cooked lentils, drained and mashed (see Note, page 86)

3   tablespoons capers, drained

⅓ cup plain nonfat yogurt

2   tablespoons tomato paste

1   large egg, lightly beaten

¾ teaspoon dried oregano

½ teaspoon dried thyme

½ teaspoon ground allspice

½ teaspoon salt

¼ teaspoon freshly ground pepper

Tomato-Caper Sauce (recipe follows) for serving

Kalamata olives for garnish

Fresh mint leaves for garnish

Preheat the oven to 350°F. In a large bowl, combine all the ingredients except the sauce, olives, and mint and mix well. Turn the mixture into a lightly sprayed or oiled 9-by-5-inch loaf pan and gently pat down. Bake until the loaf is firm and the top is lightly browned, about 1 hour. Let stand in the pan for 5 to 10 minutes before serving. Remove the loaf from the pan and transfer to a platter. Pour the hot Tomato-Caper Sauce over and garnish with the olives and mint leaves.

TOMATO-CAPER SAUCE

1 can (8 ounces) tomato sauce

1 tablespoon capers, drained and lightly crushed

1 tablespoon chopped fresh mint

1 tablespoon fresh lemon juice

¼ teaspoon dried oregano

⅛ teaspoon sugar

In a small saucepan over medium heat, combine all the ingredients and simmer until the flavors are blended, about 5 minutes. Serve hot.

makes about 1 cup

MOROCCAN MEATLOAF

Moroccan seasonings are featured in this fantastic meatloaf with exotic flavors. To carry out the theme, serve a side dish of Couscous and Pine Nuts (page 103) and a colorful garnish of citrus fruit.

Serves 6

1 pound ground turkey or chicken

½ pound ground lamb

½ cup chopped green bell pepper

½ cup chopped zucchini, drained and patted dry with a paper towel

2 garlic cloves, minced

¼ cup chopped green onions (including some tender green tops), sliced

1 cup dried whole-wheat bread crumbs

¼ cup fresh orange juice

1 large egg, lightly beaten

½ teaspoon ground coriander

½ teaspoon ground cumin

¼ teaspoon ground ginger

½ teaspoon paprika

¼ teaspoon fennel seeds

½ teaspoon ground cinnamon

½ teaspoon salt

¼ teaspoon freshly ground pepper

½ orange, peeled and sliced

½ lemon, peeled and sliced

Mint leaves for garnish

Preheat the oven to 350°F. In a large bowl, combine all the ingredients except the orange and lemon slices and mint leaves, and mix well. Turn the mixture into a lightly sprayed or oiled 9-by-5-inch loaf pan and gently pat down. Bake until the loaf is firm and the top is lightly browned, about 45 minutes. Lay the orange and lemon slices alternately on top of the loaf, overlapping slightly and bake until the fruit slices are warmed and juicy, about 15 minutes longer. Let stand in the pan for 5 to 10 minutes before serving. Remove the loaf from the pan and slice to serve. Garnish with the mint leaves.

GREEK STUFFED MEATLOAF *with tzatziki*

A combination of succulent lamb and flavorful pork is made   *Serves 4 to 6*
into a savory meatloaf with an outstanding spinach and feta
cheese filling. Serve with Tzatziki, a traditional Greek cucumber
sauce, and Toasted Pita Wedges. At one of our tasting parties
for my computer company, this meatloaf was the favorite.

1	pound ground lamb
½	pound ground pork sausage
¼	cup chopped yellow onion
¼	cup chopped red bell pepper
1	garlic clove, minced
¾	cup coarse dried bread crumbs
½	cup plain nonfat yogurt
1	large egg, lightly beaten
1	tablespoon fresh lemon juice
½	teaspoon dried oregano
1	tablespoon chopped fresh dill
	or 1 teaspoon dried dill weed
½	teaspoon salt
¼	teaspoon freshly ground pepper

Spinach Filling (page 76)
Mint leaves for garnish
Kalamata olives for garnish
Tzatziki (page 76) for serving
Toasted Pita Wedges (page 76)
   for serving

continued

NOTE: Pita, *also called pocket bread, is a*
Middle Eastern flat bread made of white
or whole-wheat flour. Cut in half, the pockets
are perfect for stuffing with a filling as a
sandwich. Serving them toasted or untoasted
makes a special bread for hors d'oeuvres
or for dipping. Here the pita triangles are
enhanced with the flavorful garlic oil.

GREEK STUFFED MEATLOAF WITH TZATZIKI

continued

Preheat the oven to 350°F. In a large bowl, combine all the ingredients except the filling, mint leaves, olives, Tzatziki, and pita wedges and mix well. Turn half of the mixture into a lightly sprayed or oiled 9-by-5-inch loaf pan and gently pat down. Spread the filling on top leaving a ½-inch border. Add the remaining meat mixture and pat down. Bake until the meatloaf is firm and the top is lightly browned, about 1 hour. Let stand in the pan for 5 to 10 minutes before serving. Remove the loaf from the pan and slice to serve. Garnish with the mint leaves and olives and serve with the Tzatziki and Toasted Pita Wedges.

SPINACH FILLING

½ package (5 ounces) frozen spinach, thawed and squeezed dry

½ cup crumbled feta cheese

2 tablespoons chopped sun-dried tomatoes, packed in oil, drained

1 garlic clove, minced

¼ teaspoon dried dill

¼ teaspoon salt

In a medium bowl, mix together all the ingredients.

makes about ¾ cup

TOASTED PITA WEDGES

¼ cup olive oil

2 garlic cloves, minced

3 pita pockets

In a small bowl, mix together the olive oil and garlic and let stand for 15 minutes. Preheat the oven to 300°F. Cut the pitas in half and cut each half into 4 wedges. Open the wedges, split them into quarters, and place, smooth-side down, on a baking sheet. Brush with garlic oil and bake until slightly browned, about 15 minutes. Let cool on a rack.

makes 24 wedges

TZATZIKI

1 cup plain nonfat yogurt, drained

½ cup finely chopped cucumber, peeled, halved, seeded, and patted dry with a paper towel

1 garlic clove, minced

1 tablespoon chopped fresh dill or ½ teaspoon dried dill

1 tablespoon chopped fresh mint

¼ teaspoon salt

¼ teaspoon freshly ground pepper

In a small bowl, combine all the ingredients and mix well. Cover and refrigerate until ready to serve.

makes about 2 cups

MEATLOAF ASIAN *style*

Two popular Asian flavors are introduced in this great-tasting meatloaf.   *Serves 6*
Soy sauce is a dark, salty sauce made by fermenting boiled soybeans and
roasted wheat or barley. Hoisin sauce is a thick, reddish-brown sauce that
is sweet and spicy. It is a mixture of soybeans, garlic, chile peppers, and
various spices. These ingredients go into a flavorful sauce used as a topping
on the meatloaf. Wasabi is the Japanese version of horseradish, and should
be used sparingly.

1   pound ground beef
½   pound ground pork
½   cup chopped yellow onion
½   cup finely chopped celery
1   garlic clove, minced
1   large egg, lightly beaten
2   tablespoons soy sauce
1   tablespoon hoisin sauce
½   teaspoon salt
¼   teaspoon freshly ground
      pepper
3   cups cooked long-grain white
      rice, divided (see Note)
      Soy-Hoisin Glaze (recipe
      follows)
      Wasabi for serving (optional)

Preheat the oven to 350°F. In a large bowl, combine all the ingredients except 2 cups of the rice, the glaze, and the wasabi and mix well. Turn the mixture into a lightly sprayed or oiled 9-by-5-inch loaf pan and gently pat down. Bake for 45 minutes. Spread the Soy-Hoisin Glaze on top of the loaf and bake until the loaf is firm and the top is lightly browned, and the sauce is bubbly, about 15 minutes longer. Let stand in the pan for 5 to 10 minutes before serving. Remove the loaf from the pan and slice to serve. Serve with the remaining rice and the wasabi, if desired.

NOTE: **To make rice,** *in a medium saucepan over medium heat, combine 1 cup long-grain white rice and 2¼ cups chicken broth or water. Bring to a boil, then reduce heat to low and simmer, covered, until the rice is tender, about 20 minutes. Fluff with a fork before serving.*

SOY-HOISIN GLAZE

¼   *cup soy sauce*
1   *tablespoon hoisin sauce*
1   *tablespoon ketchup*

In a small bowl, whisk together all the ingredients.
makes about ⅓ cup

BILL'S THAI MEATLOAF *with chili sauce*

Serves 6

After a trip to Thailand, my Chronicle editor and friend, Bill LeBlond, was inspired by the cuisine of the country and developed this meatloaf for the book. He added Thai chili sauce for just a touch of spicy sweetness and a colorful topping. His stepson, Patrick, said it was the best meatloaf he ever had. Thai chili sauce is available in Asian markets or the Asian foods section of most supermarkets.

2   slices white bread, torn into small pieces

¼   cup whole milk

1   large egg, lightly beaten

1   pound ground beef

½   pound ground turkey

1   cup finely chopped yellow onion

2   garlic cloves, minced

1   tablespoon thinly sliced fresh lemongrass (trimmed; use white part only) or 1 teaspoon grated lemon zest

2   tablespoons chopped fresh cilantro

½   teaspoon salt

¼   teaspoon freshly ground pepper

¾   cup Thai chili sauce, divided

Preheat the oven to 350°F. Place the bread in a medium bowl. Add the milk and let soak for about 30 seconds. Add the remaining ingredients to the bread with ¼ cup of the Thai chili sauce and mix well. Turn the mixture into a lightly sprayed or oiled 9-by-5-inch loaf pan and gently pat down. Bake for 45 minutes. Spread the remaining ½ cup chili sauce on top of the loaf and bake until the loaf is firm and the sauce is bubbly, about 15 minutes longer. Let stand in the pan for 5 to 10 minutes before serving. Remove the loaf from the pan and slice to serve.

CURRIED MEATLOAF *with chutney topping*

Serves 6

The combination of apples and nuts with just a hint of curry adds up to a terrific meatloaf with a distinctive flavor. Serve with Couscous and Pine Nuts (page 103).

1 pound ground lamb
½ pound ground turkey
¾ cup quick-cooking oats
½ cup peeled and chopped Granny Smith apple
1 large egg, lightly beaten
¼ cup chopped unsalted peanuts
¼ cup raisins (optional)
¼ cup chicken broth
1 teaspoon curry powder, or more to taste
¼ teaspoon ground cumin
¼ teaspoon salt
¼ teaspoon freshly ground pepper
½ cup chutney (such as Major Grey's)

Preheat the oven to 350°F. In a large bowl, combine all the ingredients except the chutney and mix well. Turn the mixture into a lightly sprayed or oiled 9-by-5-inch loaf pan and gently pat down. Bake for 45 minutes. Spread the chutney on top of the loaf and bake until the loaf is firm and the chutney is bubbly, about 15 minutes longer. Let stand in the pan for 5 to 10 minutes before serving. Remove the loaf from the pan and slice to serve.

OTHER LOAVES

Add variety to your repertoire with some
of these wonderful loaves using poultry,
seafood, vegetables, pasta, grains, and nuts in
tantalizing combinations. If you think a loaf
needs beef, you will be pleasantly surprised.

Included are:
- *Turkey Loaf with Cranberry Sauce*
- *Julie's Brown Rice Loaf*
- *Macaroni and Cheese Loaf*

*and other healthful loaves for vegetarians
and nonvegetarians alike.*

TURKEY LOAF WITH *cranberry sauce*

Serves 4

Lean, mild ground turkey makes a delicious loaf if it is well-seasoned. This version, topped with a colorful cranberry sauce for flavor and color is a timely loaf to serve during the holidays. Bake sweet potatoes alongside for an easy weeknight dinner.

1½ pounds ground turkey

¼ cup finely chopped yellow onion

½ cup peeled and grated carrot

¼ cup finely chopped celery

1 cup coarse dried bread crumbs

½ cup chicken broth

½ teaspoon dried sage

½ teaspoon poultry seasoning

1 large egg, lightly beaten

½ teaspoon salt

¼ teaspoon freshly ground pepper

1 cup homemade or canned cranberry sauce, slightly drained, at room temperature

Fresh sage leaves for garnish

In a large bowl, combine all the ingredients except the cranberry sauce and sage leaves and mix well. Turn the mixture into a lightly sprayed or oiled 9-by-5-inch loaf pan and gently pat down. Bake until the loaf is firm and the top is lightly browned, about 1 hour. Spread the cranberry sauce on top of the loaf and let stand in the pan for 5 to 10 minutes before serving. Remove the loaf from the pan and transfer to a platter. Garnish with sage leaves.

TURKEY-VEGETABLE LOAF

Serves 6 *Watching your diet? This low-fat loaf made with lean ground turkey and fresh vegetables is a perfect choice. Serve with baked sweet potatoes and cranberry sauce.*

1   cup diced yellow onion

4   ounces mushrooms, cleaned, trimmed, and chopped

1   cup diced broccoli florets

½   cup diced green bell pepper

1   cup peeled and grated carrots

¼   cup chopped fresh parsley

1   garlic clove, minced

1¼ pounds ground turkey

¾   cup quick-cooking oats

¼   cup ketchup

2   tablespoons soy sauce

1   large egg or 2 egg whites, lightly beaten

1   teaspoon poultry seasoning

¾   teaspoon salt

¼   teaspoon freshly ground pepper
Homemade or canned cranberry sauce at room temperature, for serving

Preheat the oven to 350°F. In a medium saucepan over high heat, combine the onion, mushrooms, broccoli, bell pepper, and carrots with salted water to cover. Bring to a boil and cook for about 2 minutes. Drain well and transfer to a large bowl. Add the remaining ingredients except the cranberry sauce and mix well. Turn the mixture into a lightly sprayed or oiled 9-by-5-inch loaf pan and gently pat down. Bake until the loaf is firm and the top is lightly browned, about 1 hour. Let stand in the pan for 5 to 10 minutes before serving. Remove the loaf from the pan, transfer to a platter, and slice to serve. Serve with the cranberry sauce.

SALMON LOAF *with lemon-dill sauce*

Fresh cooked salmon is preferred for this loaf, but canned salmon can also be used. Serve with refreshing Lemon-Dill Sauce and a side dish of fresh sautéed spinach.

2¼ cups fresh cooked salmon, flaked, or 3 cans (6 ounces each) boneless and skinless pink salmon, drained and flaked

1 cup finely crushed saltines, about 20

¼ cup chopped yellow onion

1 large egg, lightly beaten

¼ cup whole milk

1 tablespoon fresh lemon juice

1 teaspoon grated lemon zest

3 tablespoons chopped fresh parsley

¾ teaspoon dried dill weed

¼ teaspoon salt

¼ teaspoon freshly ground pepper

Dill sprigs for garnish

Lemon-Dill Sauce (recipe follows) for serving

Preheat the oven to 350°F. In a medium bowl, combine all the ingredients except the dill sprigs and sauce and mix well. Turn the mixture into a lightly sprayed or oiled 9-by-5-inch loaf pan and gently pat down. Bake until the loaf is firm and the top is lightly browned, about 40 minutes. Let stand in the pan for 5 to 10 minutes before serving. Remove the loaf from the pan and slice to serve. Garnish with the dill sprigs. Pass the Lemon-Dill Sauce in a small bowl.

Serves 4

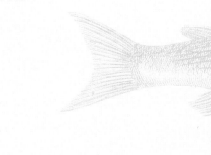

LEMON-DILL SAUCE

¼ cup mayonnaise

¼ cup plain nonfat yogurt or sour cream

1 tablespoon fresh lemon juice

½ teaspoon dried dill

¼ teaspoon salt

½ teaspoon sugar

In a small bowl, mix together all the ingredients. Serve at room temperature.

makes about ½ cup

LENTIL-MUSHROOM-WALNUT LOAF

Serves 4 to 6 *Great-tasting ingredients add up to a nutritious and satisfying meatless entrée. The lentils provide texture and substance. Add a tossed green salad to round out the menu.*

3 cups cooked lentils, drained (see Note)

½ cup chopped yellow onion

2 garlic cloves, minced

1 pound mushrooms, chopped

½ cup chopped walnuts

½ cup quick-cooking oats

2 large eggs, lightly beaten

1 tablespoon Dijon mustard

1 teaspoon Worcestershire sauce

1 teaspoon soy sauce

¼ teaspoon salt

¼ teaspoon freshly ground pepper

1½ cups shredded mozzarella cheese

Preheat the oven to 350°F. In a large bowl, combine all the ingredients except the cheese and mix well. Turn the mixture into a lightly sprayed or oiled 8-by-8-inch glass baking dish and gently pat down. Bake until the loaf is firm and the top is lightly browned, about 40 minutes. Sprinkle the cheese on top and bake until the cheese is melted, about 10 minutes longer. Let stand in the dish for 5 to 10 minutes before serving. Cut into squares and serve from the baking dish.

NOTE: To make the lentils, sort 1¼ cup dried lentils. In a medium saucepan over high heat, combine the lentils with 2 cups water. Do not add salt. Bring to a boil. Reduce the heat to low and simmer, covered, until the lentils are tender, about 35 minutes.

JULIE'S **BROWN RICE** LOAF

Brown rice, with its nutty flavor and chewy texture,
makes an appealing base for this savory loaf when
combined with nuts, seeds, cheese, and vegetables.
Even my grandkids liked it! Serve with sliced tomatoes
drizzled with balsamic vinegar and hard-cooked
egg quarters.

Serves 4 to 6

1	cup brown rice, cooked as directed on the package (3 cups cooked)
2	cups shredded Cheddar cheese
4	large eggs, lightly beaten
1	cup chopped yellow onion
1	cup peeled and grated carrots
½	cup dried bread crumbs
¼	cup chopped walnuts
¼	cup chopped sunflower seeds
¼	cup sesame seeds
1	teaspoon dried basil
½	teaspoon salt
¼	teaspoon freshly ground pepper
	Ketchup for serving

Preheat the oven to 350°F. In a large bowl, combine all the ingredients except the ketchup and mix well. Turn the mixture into a lightly sprayed or oiled 9-by-5-inch loaf pan and gently pat down. Bake until the loaf is firm and the top is lightly browned, about 1 hour. Let stand in the pan for 5 to 10 minutes before serving. Remove the loaf from the pan and slice to serve. Serve with the ketchup.

MACARONI AND CHEESE LOAF

Serves 6 *If you like macaroni and cheese, you'll love this loaf. It is good served plain as a side dish or, if you wish, with Mom's Tomato Sauce (page 23) for a main course.*

1 cup dried elbow macaroni, broken up (see Note), cooked as directed on the package and drained

4 to 6 green onions, including some tender green tops, sliced

½ cup chopped pimiento peppers, drained

⅓ cup chopped fresh parsley

1½ cups shredded Cheddar cheese, divided

1 cup whole milk

1 large egg, lightly beaten

¼ teaspoon dried thyme

1 teaspoon salt

¼ teaspoon freshly ground pepper

1 tablespoon butter, melted

½ cup coarse dried bread crumbs

Preheat the oven to 400°F. In a medium bowl, mix together the macaroni, green onions, pimientos, and parsley. In a lightly sprayed or oiled 9-by-5-inch loaf pan or 8-by-8-inch baking dish, add half of the macaroni mixture, followed by half of the cheese. Repeat the layers. In a medium bowl, whisk together the milk, egg, thyme, salt, and pepper. Pour the milk mixture over the loaf. Mix the melted butter with the bread crumbs and sprinkle on top. Bake until the crumbs are browned, about 35 minutes. Let stand in the pan for 10 to 15 minutes before serving. Remove the loaf from the pan and slice to serve, or cut into squares if using a baking dish.

NOTE: *Place the macaroni in a plastic bag and break it up into large, coarse pieces with a rolling pin or jar. Do not crush completely.*

SIDE DISHES

Side dishes should complement the meatloaf and add interest to the meal. Potatoes are the traditional accompaniment to serve with meatloaf, so this chapter offers a good selection of everyday popular choices. Rice and pasta fit the bill similarly, and a few simple but impressive recipes for these basics are featured here as well.

Keep in mind that side dishes for ethnic loaves should have similar spices and flavors to carry out the regional theme.

Mix and match side dishes like:

· *Fluffy Mashed Potatoes*

· *Hash Browns*

· *Roasted Rosemary Potatoes with Parmesan Cheese*

· *Pecan Rice*

· *Couscous and Pine Nuts*

Remember, for an easy meal, simply baking potatoes alongside the meatloaf while you toss a crisp green salad completes your menu.

FLUFFY MASHED POTATOES

Serves 6   Mashed potatoes have always been associated with meatloaf as a natural accompaniment. Additional ingredients can be added for variety; see the variations below.

4   **medium russet potatoes (about 2½ pounds), peeled and quartered**
¾   **teaspoon salt, divided**
½   **to ¾ cup half-and-half or whole milk**
4   **tablespoons unsalted butter, at room temperature, divided**
¼   **teaspoon freshly ground pepper**

In a large saucepan over high heat, combine the potatoes with water to cover and bring to a boil. Add ¼ teaspoon of the salt, reduce the heat to medium low, and simmer until tender, about 20 minutes. Drain well. Return the potatoes to the warm pan, add ½ cup of the half-and-half, and beat with an electric mixer or potato masher until smooth. Use additional half-and-half or milk if needed for desired consistency. Cut 2 tablespoons of the butter into small pieces and beat into the potatoes. Add the remaining ½ teaspoon salt and the pepper and fluff with a fork. Transfer to a warmed bowl, dot the remaining butter on top, and serve immediately.

VARIATIONS

for horseradish mashed potatoes
add 1 tablespoon prepared horseradish sauce, or more to taste, to the mashed potatoes.

for garlic mashed potatoes
cook 2 or 3 peeled garlic cloves with the potatoes and mash with the potatoes.

for Dijon mashed potatoes
add 1 tablespoon Dijon mustard to the potatoes.

SMASHED NEW POTATOES *with cilantro*

Serves 4 to 6 *Smashed potatoes are barely mashed and should be chunky. Unpeeled new red potatoes are a good choice. Here, cilantro is added for a fresh taste and color to complement Tex-Mex Meatloaf (page 61).*

14 to 16 small red potatoes (about 1½ pounds, 1½-inch diameter), unpeeled and scrubbed

¾ to 1 cup buttermilk

¼ teaspoon salt

¼ teaspoon freshly ground pepper

½ cup chopped fresh cilantro, parsley, or chives

1 tablespoon unsalted butter, at room temperature (optional)

In a large saucepan over high heat, combine the potatoes with water to cover and bring to a boil. Reduce the heat to medium-low and simmer until tender, about 20 minutes. Drain well. Return the potatoes to the warm pan and add ¾ cup of the buttermilk and mash with a potato masher or large fork until chunky. Use additional buttermilk if needed for the desired consistency. Stir in the salt, pepper, cilantro, and butter, if using.

STEAMED NEW POTATOES *with fresh basil*

New potatoes from the garden or produce stand are a summer   *Serves 4 to 6*
delight. Simply steamed and tossed with butter, fresh, pungent
basil, salt, and pepper, they are ready to enjoy. For variety, use a
mixture of red and white potatoes.

1 **pound small new potatoes (about 1-inch diameter), unpeeled and well-scrubbed**

2 **tablespoons unsalted butter, at room temperature**

2 **tablespoons chopped fresh basil**

¼ **teaspoon salt**

¼ **teaspoon freshly ground pepper**

Place the potatoes in a steamer rack set in a saucepan over boiling water. Reduce the heat to medium-low and cook, covered, until tender, 15 to 20 minutes. Transfer to a bowl and toss with the butter, basil, salt, and pepper.

TWICE-BAKED POTATOES

Serves 4   *Time to reintroduce this old standby, which has been a favorite among all ages for years. The potatoes can be baked and prepared ahead, and then baked the second time before serving. (If refrigerated, bring to room temperature before baking.) These delicious potatoes make a good accompaniment to serve with any meatloaf.*

4   large russet potatoes (about 2 ½ pounds), unpeeled, scrubbed, dried, and rubbed with vegetable oil

¼   cup sour cream

¼   cup whole milk

½   teaspoon salt

¼   teaspoon freshly ground pepper

1   cup shredded Cheddar cheese

4   green onions, including some tender green tops, chopped (optional)

Preheat the oven to 350°F. Prick the potatoes with a fork or the tip of a sharp knife several times. Bake until tender, about 1 hour. Remove from the oven and let cool slightly, then cut each potato in half lengthwise and scoop the pulp into a bowl, leaving the shell intact. With an electric mixer or a potato masher, beat or mash the pulp. Add the sour cream, milk, salt, and pepper and beat until fluffy. Stir in the cheese and green onions, if using. Spoon the potato mixture back into the shells. Place on a baking sheet and bake until heated through and lightly browned, 20 to 25 minutes.

VARIATION

for Mexican-style twice-baked potatoes, use pepper Jack cheese instead of Cheddar cheese. Add ¼ cup salsa and sprinkle with chopped fresh cilantro instead of the green onions.

ROASTED ROSEMARY POTATOES WITH *parmesan cheese*

Serves 4

Crisp on the outside and creamy on the inside, these potatoes make a good accompaniment to Tuscan Meatloaf (page 67).

1 tablespoon olive oil

2 teaspoons coarse salt

¼ teaspoon freshly ground pepper

2 tablespoons chopped fresh rosemary or 1 teaspoon dried rosemary

4 medium, unpeeled Yukon Gold potatoes (about 1¼ pounds), scrubbed and quartered lengthwise into wedges

Freshly grated Parmesan cheese for sprinkling

Preheat the oven to 400°F. In an 8-by-8-inch glass baking dish, mix the olive oil, salt, pepper, and rosemary. Add the potato wedges and toss to coat. Bake until tender and crisp, about 40 minutes, turning once. Sprinkle with the Parmesan and serve immediately.

OVEN FRENCH FRIES

Serves 4 to 6   Hungry for French fries? Bake them in the oven with very little oil and you can forget the calories. Roasted Garlic Mayonnaise is a must for dipping. Serve with Super Cheeseburger Loaf (page 29).

4   large russet potatoes (about 2½ pounds)

3   to 4 tablespoons vegetable oil
Seasoning salt (such as Lawry's)
Freshly ground pepper
Roasted Garlic Mayonnaise (recipe follows) for serving

Preheat the oven to 425°F. Peel the potatoes and place in a large bowl with water to cover for 30 minutes to remove excess starch. Drain and pat dry with paper towels. Cut the potatoes lengthwise into ¼-inch-thick slices, then cut into ¼-inch-wide strips. In a bowl, toss the potatoes with the oil. Arrange the potatoes in a single layer on a baking sheet. Bake, uncovered, for 15 minutes. Turn over and sprinkle generously with the seasoning salt and pepper. Bake until golden brown, about 10 minutes longer. Serve immediately.

ROASTED GARLIC MAYONNAISE

This is also good on vegetables and steak.

1   garlic head, papery skin removed, unpeeled and head left intact

2   teaspoons olive oil

1   cup mayonnaise
Juice of ½ a lemon
Salt and freshly ground pepper to taste

Preheat the oven to 400°F. Trim about ½ inch from the top of the garlic head. Place on a square of aluminum foil and drizzle with the olive oil, allowing it to flow in between the cloves. Wrap tightly in the foil. Bake until soft, about 30 minutes. Let cool, then squeeze out the pulp into a medium bowl. Add the mayonnaise, lemon juice, salt, and pepper and mix well.

makes about 1 cup

GRILLED **CHEESY POTATO** WEDGES

Serves 4

These are fun to make in the summer on the grill to serve with the barbecued meatloaf recipe on page 38 or other grilled meats.

3   medium russet potatoes (about 2 pounds), unpeeled, scrubbed, and halved lengthwise
     Olive oil for brushing
     Paprika for sprinkling
     Coarse salt and freshly ground pepper
1½ cups shredded Cheddar cheese

In a medium saucepan over high heat, combine the potatoes with water to cover and bring to a boil. Reduce the heat to medium-low and simmer until almost tender, about 15 minutes. Drain and cool under running cold water. (The potatoes can be made ahead up to this point.) Quarter each half and transfer to a lightly sprayed or oiled foil pan. Brush with olive oil. Sprinkle with paprika, salt, and pepper, then top with the cheese. Prepare a fire in a charcoal grill or preheat a gas grill to medium. Place the pan holding the potatoes on the grill and cook until the potatoes are crisp and hot and the cheese is melted, about 15 minutes. Serve immediately.

HASH **BROWNS**

Serves 4

Hash browns are finely chopped or grated potatoes fried in oil or bacon fat. For convenience, you can buy them frozen, but I think you'll appreciate the difference when you make your own with this easy recipe. Serve with the Truck-Stop Meatloaf recipe on page 24.

3 large russet potatoes
   (about 2 pounds), peeled
5 or 6 green onions, including
   some tender green tops,
   sliced (optional)
3 to 4 tablespoons vegetable oil,
   bacon drippings, or shortening
   Coarse salt and freshly ground
   pepper

Using a food processor fitted with the shredding blade or a handheld grater, grate the potatoes. Place the grated potatoes in a bowl of cold water to prevent discoloring while you finish grating. Drain and pat dry. Return to the bowl and stir in the green onions, if using. In a medium non-stick skillet over medium heat, warm 3 tablespoons of the oil. Spread the potatoes in the skillet and press down with a spatula. Sprinkle generously with salt and pepper. Cook until the bottom is browned, about 5 minutes. Do not stir. Using a spatula, turn the potatoes. Add more oil to the pan, if needed. Cook until the second side is crisp, about 5 minutes longer.

BOURBON SWEET POTATOES *with pecans*

Pair this flavorful side dish with Ham and Pork Meatloaf with — *Serves 6*
Honey-Mustard Sauce (page 48) or Turkey Loaf with Cranberry
Sauce (page 82) for a company dinner. This dish is best with
the yellow variety of sweet potato, not the deep orange types,
though any sweet potato will be fine.

4	medium sweet potatoes (about 2 pounds), unpeeled and scrubbed
¼	cup (½ stick) unsalted butter
½	cup firmly packed brown sugar
¼	cup water
¼	teaspoon salt
1	to 2 tablespoons bourbon
¼	cup chopped pecans

Preheat the oven to 350°F. Prick the potatoes with a fork or the tip of a sharp knife several times. Bake until tender, about 1 hour. Remove from the oven and let cool slightly, then peel and cut each potato lengthwise into quarters. Place in a lightly sprayed or oiled 8-by-10-inch baking dish. Meanwhile, in a small saucepan over medium-heat, combine the butter, brown sugar, water, and salt and stir until the butter is melted and the sugar is dissolved, 2 to 3 minutes. Remove from the heat and add the bourbon. Pour the mixture over the potatoes. Bake, uncovered, for 30 minutes. Turn and sprinkle with the pecans. Bake until bubbly, 10 to 15 minutes longer.

RED AND GREEN RICE

This is an easy version of a **Serves 4**
colorful rice dish I enjoyed
in Mexico. It makes a natural
accompaniment to any
Mexican or Southwestern dish.

1 cup long-grain white rice
½ cup chopped white onion
1 garlic clove, minced
2 medium tomatoes,
    chopped and drained
1 can (4 ounces) diced
    green chiles, drained
2 cups chicken broth
¼ teaspoon ground cumin
¼ teaspoon dried oregano
¼ teaspoon salt
¼ cup chopped fresh
    cilantro or parsley

Preheat the oven to 350°F.
In a lightly sprayed or oiled
2-quart casserole, mix
together all the ingredients
except the cilantro. Bake,
covered, until the rice is tender
and the liquid is absorbed,
about 45 minutes. Sprinkle
with the cilantro and serve
immediately.

BAKED POLENTA WITH *parmesan cheese*

Polenta, a staple of northern Italy, is coarse-grind cornmeal,
cooked and eaten soft as a side dish, baked and cut into
squares, or cooled until firm and then fried. This baked version
is an easy way to make creamy polenta for an accompaniment
to Italian Meatloaf (page 69), other Mediterranean loaves, or
any Italian-themed meat dish.

1 cup polenta
4 cups water
½ teaspoon salt
1 tablespoon unsalted
    butter, cut into bits
½ cup freshly grated
    Parmesan cheese
¼ cup sour cream

Preheat the oven to 350°F. In a
lightly sprayed or oiled 8-by-
8-inch glass baking dish, mix
the polenta with the water, salt,
and butter. Bake, uncovered, for
40 minutes. Stir in the cheese
and sour cream and bake until
firm, about 10 minutes longer.
Remove from the oven and let
stand for 5 to 10 minutes before
serving.

Serves 6

LEMON **ORZO**

Orzo is a small, quick-cooking, delicate Italian pasta shaped like rice and often used as a substitute for that grain. It is ideal for soups, stews, and casseroles. Here, the lemon adds a refreshing flavor that complements seafood and vegetable dishes.

 Serves 4

3⅓ cups water

1 teaspoon salt

1 cup dried orzo

1 teaspoon grated lemon zest

1 teaspoon fresh lemon juice

2 tablespoons chopped fresh parsley

1 teaspoon olive oil

In a medium saucepan over high heat, bring the water to a boil. Add the salt and orzo. Reduce the heat to medium and simmer, uncovered, until tender, 10 to 12 minutes, stirring occasionally. Drain, add the remaining ingredients, and mix well. Serve immediately.

PECAN RICE

Serves 4

This simple rice dish goes great with Cajun Meatloaf (page 60), but is an all-purpose side dish for many loaves. If preferred, walnuts can be used instead of pecans.

2¼ cups chicken broth

1   cup uncooked long-grain
      white rice

¼   teaspoon salt

1   tablespoon butter

⅓   cup chopped pecans

¼   cup chopped fresh parsley

In a medium saucepan over medium-high heat, bring the broth to a boil. Stir in the rice and salt. Reduce the heat to medium-low and cook, covered, until the rice is tender and the liquid is absorbed, about 20 minutes. Add the butter, pecans, and parsley and fluff with a fork.

COUSCOUS AND PINE NUTS

Couscous, a tiny grain-like pasta made from semolina flour, is the basis of many Middle Eastern dishes. It is very versatile and can be served as a side dish, salad, or, with meat added, as a main course. It is popular because it has no fat, no cholesterol, and takes only minutes to prepare. Pine nuts come from the cones of certain varieties of pine tree; they can be purchased in bulk or in packages. They make a unique contribution to this dish. Serve with Moroccan Meatloaf (page 73).

Serves 4

1½ cups chicken broth or water

1½ cups couscous

6 green onions, including some tender green tops, sliced

⅓ cup pine nuts, toasted (see Note)

3 tablespoons chopped fresh parsley

2 tablespoons chopped fresh mint leaves (optional)

2 tablespoons unsalted butter, at room temperature

¼ teaspoon salt

¼ teaspoon freshly ground pepper

In a medium saucepan over high heat, bring the chicken broth to a boil. Stir in the couscous and remove from the heat. Cover and let stand until the couscous is tender and the broth is absorbed, about 10 minutes. Add the green onions, pine nuts, parsley, mint (if using), and butter. Season with the salt and pepper and fluff with a fork. Serve immediately, or keep warm in a pan over hot water until ready to serve.

*NOTE: **To toast pine nuts,** place them in a small, dry skillet over medium-high heat. Stir constantly until they begin to brown, about 2 minutes. Watch carefully, as they burn quickly. Transfer to a plate immediately.*

ABOUT THE **AUTHOR**

MARYANA VOLLSTEDT is a native of Oregon and graduated from Oregon State University with a degree in Home Economics. In 1952 she and her husband, Reed, started Reed and Cross, a small nursery and garden center that grew into a retail complex including a landscape service, a florist, a gift shop, gourmet cookware, a wine shop, and a deli. This is where Maryana started her writing career in the mid-1960s, by authoring the first cookbook and manual for the Kamado barbecue. She continued to write, and self-published 15 other cookbooks on a variety of subjects.

The Vollstedts sold the store in 1979 to travel and pursue other interests. Since 1995, Maryana has written seven best-selling cookbooks, all published by Chronicle Books. She also writes a bimonthly food column called "What's for Dinner?" for her local newspaper, the *Eugene Register-Guard*. Maryana lives with her husband in Eugene, Oregon, where she continues to write cookbooks. She can be reached through her Web site at WWW.MARYANAVOLLSTEDT.COM.

INDEX

TABLE OF *equivalents*

The exact equivalents in the following tables have been rounded for convenience.

LIQUID/DRY MEASURES

u.s.	metric
¼ teaspoon	1.25 milliliters
½ teaspoon	2.5 milliliters
1 teaspoon	5 milliliters
1 tablespoon (3 teaspoons)	15 milliliters
1 fluid ounce (2 tablespoons)	30 milliliters
¼ cup	60 milliliters
⅓ cup	80 milliliters
½ cup	120 milliliters
1 cup	240 milliliters
1 pint (2 cups)	480 milliliters
1 quart (4 cups; 32 ounces)	960 milliliters
1 gallon (4 quarts)	3.84 liters
1 ounce (by weight)	28 grams
1 pound	448 grams
2.2 pounds	1 kilogram

LENGTHS

u.s.	metric
⅛ inch	3 millimeters
¼ inch	6 millimeters
½ inch	12 millimeters
1 inch	2.5 centimeters

OVEN TEMPERATURES

fahrenheit	celsius	gas
250	120	½
275	140	1
300	150	2
325	160	3
350	180	4
375	190	5
400	200	6
425	220	7
450	230	8
475	240	9
500	260	10